THE INFLUENCE OF HORACE ON THE CHIEF ENGLISH POETS OF THE NINETEENTH CENTURY

THE INFLUENCE OF HORACE ON THE CHIEF ENGLISH POETS OF THE NINETEENTH CENTURY

BY

MARY REBECCA THAYER

NEW YORK / RUSSELL & RUSSELL

FIRST PUBLISHED IN 1916

REISSUED, 1968, BY RUSSELL & RUSSELL

A DIVISION OF ATHENEUM HOUSE, INC.

BY ARRANGEMENT WITH CORNELL UNIVERSITY PRESS

L. C. CATALOG CARD NO: 67-18297

PRINTED IN THE UNITED STATES OF AMERICA

TO

PROFESSOR LANE COOPER

IN GRATITUDE FOR HIS ENCOURAGEMENT,
COUNSEL, AND AID

PREFACE

The following study, in substantially its present form, was prepared as a doctoral dissertation while I was holding a fellowship in English at Cornell University; it was undertaken in the belief that the relation between English literature and other literatures, especially those of classic Greece and Rome, though its existence is readily admitted by almost every one, has not been sufficiently investigated and ascertained in detail. Such general surveys as Tucker's *Foreign Debt of English Literature* can in the nature of things but glide over the surface of the vast field before them; and the careful elaboration of particular instances such as Reinsch's study of Horace and Ben Jonson (see below, page 108) is rare. So far as I am aware, no one has hitherto attempted to do for any single Greek or Latin author, in relation to our literature, what Paget Toynbee has done for Dante (*Dante in English Literature*, London, 1909); yet in the case of several of the Roman writers, at any rate, far more material might be collected than for Dante. Indeed, it is perhaps the very wealth of material that holds many students aloof from the necessary investigations; too few are blest with the vision characteristic of Browning's grammarian. But, even so, we may realize that every rigorous comparison of an ancient with a modern author, or with a group of modern authors, will constitute a necessary addition, however small, to the lofty structure which we desire to see ideally complete.

My choice of Horace as the centre of my work was in part determined by my own predilection, but more by the feeling that, when all is said, he has been the most popular Latin poet with English writers. The claims of Virgil and Ovid, of course, are very strong; yet I think that Horace can more than hold his own with either of these. I selected the nineteenth century on the ground that there would be an especial interest in learning, through one set of particulars, what sort of influence the ancient classics had on an age which, as is generally supposed, is marked by a tendency to break away from them. But I expect before long to follow Horace through other periods, and to observe his influence in other English authors. My hope is that, singly, or combined with the work of others, my studies may at some time result in a substantial volume which may fairly be called 'Horace in English Literature.'

I am glad to take this opportunity of expressing my gratitude to all who have aided me in the prosecution of my study. A list of the books I have consulted will be found at the end of the work (pp. 107-109); but I should like to speak in particular of *Classical Echoes in Tennyson*, by W. P. Mustard, of Johns Hopkins University, and of the very helpful notes in the Shorey-Laing edition of the *Odes and Epodes* of Horace. I am indebted to Professor Mustard also for two Words-worthian allusions; to Professor Lane Cooper, of Cornell University, under whose direction the work was begun, for his constant interest and his many useful suggestions; and to others who on occasion have been so good as to furnish me with valuable references.

MARY REBECCA THAYER

VASSAR COLLEGE, January 9, 1916

TABLE OF CONTENTS

INTRODUCTION

In order properly to discuss the influence of one writer upon another, it is necessary to determine as nearly as may be for what each of them stands; for the measure of real influence is, after all, the amount of sympathy which exists between the two. Therefore, prior to taking up the relation of Horace to nineteenth-century English poetry, we must endeavor to obtain a true idea of him as he shows himself to us.

The attempt to discover a man in his poems is always fascinating, but also to a greater or less extent dangerous. The reason for this is twofold: first, most poets have the faculty of merging their own identity from time to time in the imaginary men and women of whom they write, so that it is indeed Oedipus, or Francesca, or Lady Macbeth, or Paracelsus, whom we hear speaking; secondly, the eager interpreter is all too apt to forget the 'infinite variety' which goes to make up every human being, and, dwelling on certain poems, while disregarding others, to construct therefrom a caricature which the poet himself would be the last to recognize as his portrait.

From the first of these dangers Horace is not so likely to suffer; for it is true that some poets commit more of themselves to their verse than do others, and he belongs to the former class. So careful a student as the late Professor Sellar finds him one of the most self-revealing of poets; and Professor J. Wight Duff, the able historian of Latin literature, says of him: 'No Roman author except Cicero has left anything like so complete a self-revelation as Horace.'[1]

It is well for us that this is true, since there is no record of him except the brief life by Suetonius, which furnishes a mere biographical outline, but not the vastly more important details of the poet's personality. Concerning Horace there has come down to us none of the contemporary appreciation which helps us to realize even so inscrutable a figure as 'gentle Shakespeare.' It is from Horace alone that we may hope to know Horace—the friend of Virgil, the favorite of Maecenas, the protégé of Augustus, the poet of us all.

From the second danger, however, Horace suffers much. Critic after critic has taken the lighter odes, the *vers de société* which the poet

[1] *A Literary History of Rome,* p. 496.

could write so charmingly, and with them for background has painted
a picture of an amiable trifler, feeling deeply on no subject except perhaps when the ugly thought of inevitable death obtrudes itself; a
finished workman, caring far more for the polishing and setting than
for the gem itself.   Thus we find Keble saying:[1]

'I reluctantly confess myself hitherto unable to discover any peculiar and dominating spring of Horace's poetry.   In fact, I suspect his
light touch of all subjects betrays to us that he dwelt with no serious
regard on any one of them.   He professes at times a notable enthusi-
asm for the country and rural life: yet one always feels that his interest
was rather after the manner of those who merely seek recreation there
than of the country-folk themselves; that Rome was all the time in his
thoughts; that he cherished his little farm and his homely belongings,
less for their own sake than for their restful repose, their elegant hospi-
talities, and whatsoever other like attractions they offered.   In brief:
he enrolled himself . . . without misgiving in the ranks of the
Epicureans; setting before him as his sole rule of life the hope of grasp-
ing the gifts of the passing hour, whatever they might chance to be.
. . . We see, then, in him a genial gentleman, one too nearly in
sympathy with the crowd, who indulge their own bent, to be deeply
influenced by any tender regard for things far away.'

This criticism contains an element of truth.   Horace *was* an Epicurean; he *was* a genial gentleman.   But, for the rest, we surely will
not acknowledge that *carpe diem* was his 'sole rule of life,' when we
recall (to take a familiar instance) the golden mean upon which he
time and again insists; we cannot agree that he took no active interest
in country life when we read such passages as the following:

> Vivere naturae si convenienter oportet,
> Ponendaeque domo quaerenda est arca primum,
> Novistine locum potiorem rure beato?
> Est ubi plus tepeant hiemes?   . . .
> Est ubi divellat somnos minus invida cura?
> Deterius Libycis olet aut nitet herba lapillis?
> Purior in vicis aqua tendit rumpere plumbum,
> Quam quae per pronum trepidat cum murmure rivum?
> Nempe inter varias nutritur silva columnas,
> Laudaturque domus longos quae prospicit agros.
> Naturam expelles furca, tamen usque recurret;[2]

---

[1] *Lectures on Poetry*, tr. E. K. Francis, 2. 467 ff.

[2] If we are to live in accordance with nature, and first of all are to hunt for a spot to build a house, do
you know a place preferable to the prosperous country? Is there any place where the winters are milder?
Is there any place where carking care less disturbs our sleep? Does grass smell less sweet or look

and if we carefully consider the entire body of Horace's work, we must refuse to admit that he touched all subjects lightly. Rather we may accept the judgment of Sellar:[1]

'He is at once the lyrical poet, with heart and imagination responsive to the deeper meaning and lighter amusements of life, and the satirist, the moralist, and the literary critic of the age.'

The safe method, then, is to discover, if we can, for ourselves what Horace reveals of himself in his works; not, **Characteristics** be it understood, such facts of his life as that his **of Horace.** father was a freedman, and that he once narrowly escaped being struck by a falling tree, but the characteristics of the man as his poetry discloses them. And for a first descriptive epithet we may echo one of Keble's—'genial.'

Geniality, indeed, is the key-note of Horace's work. We see it in the epistles, which, though addressed to dead and gone Romans, are really, we feel, for us all; yet are not impersonal 'open letters,' but rather a delightful admission of the interested to his confidence. We see it even in his most sharply satirical passages; for virtually all students of Horace the satirist have noticed that he almost never loses his good humor—that he laughs at follies instead of railing at them. We see it in many of his lyrics, such as *Vides ut alta . . . Soracte, Integer vitae,* and *Septimi Gadis aditure mecum.* It is everywhere apparent, so that we find ourselves feeling that here is a man whom it would have been a pleasure to know and to talk with.

Yet, though nearly always good-humored, Horace is far from being always happy. There is, indeed, a sombre strain in him that frequently shows itself when we least expect.

> Diffugere nives, redeunt iam gramina campis,

he sings,

> Arboribusque comae;
> . . . .
> Gratia cum Nymphis geminisque sororibus audet
> Ducere nuda choros.

And then he adds abruptly:

> Immortalia ne speres, monet annus et almum
> Quae rapit hora diem.
> . . . .

---

less beautiful than pavements? Is water which tries to burst its pipes in the streets purer than that which hurries murmuring down its channel? Why, even among columns of variegated marble trees are tended, and a house which has a view of far-away fields is praised. You may drive out nature with a pitchfork, but she will ever return. (*Epist.* 1. 10. 12-24.)

[1] *Horace and the Elegiac Poets,* p. 3.

Damna tamen celeres reparant caelestia lunae:
Nos ubi decidimus
Quo pius Aeneas, quo dives Tullus et Ancus,
Pulvis et umbra sumus.[1]

Or again:

Solvitur acris hiems grata vice veris et Favoni.
.   .   .   .
Nunc decet aut viridi nitidum caput impedire myrto
Aut flore terrae quem ferunt solutae;
Nunc et in umbrosis Fauno decet immolare lucis,
Seu poscat agna sive malit haedo.
Pallida mors aequo pulsat pede pauperum tabernas
Regumque turris.   O beate Sesti,
Vitae summa brevis spem nos vetat incohare longam.[2]

It is in this feeling of the inevitableness of death that the melancholy of Horace usually shows itself.

The glories of our blood and state
Are shadows, not substantial things;
There is no armor against fate;
Death lays his icy hand on kings—

the thought runs throughout his poetry; and from this naturally enough follows the desire to get out of life all it has to offer.

Carpe diem, quam minimum credula postero,[3]

he again and again advises, though in varying words.   Yet that this desire for instant happiness is with him no mere unregulated impulse is evident to any reader; for perhaps the chief element of the Horatian philosophy is moderation.   The golden mean is the standard which the poet sets before himself and those who care to listen to him, and he despises alike the avarice of the miser and the extravagance of the spendthrift.   The happiness he wishes for his brief life is, then, carefully planned, and dependent upon the scrupulous balancing of desire with desire.   He carries this doctrine to its logical conclusion, and tells us: *Virtus est medium vitiorum.*   The fact that this advice to

---

[1] The snow has fled away, grass now returns to the fields, and leaves to the trees.   The Grace, with the Nymphs and her own twin sisters, ventures unrobed to lead the choric dance.   'Do not hope for immortality,' is the warning of the year and the hour which snatches from us the cheerful day.   Swift-changing moons repair their wanings; but when we have once departed to where pious Aeneas and rich Tullus and Ancus have gone before, we are but dust and shadow.   (*Carm.* 4. 7. 1-16.)

[2] Sharp winter is driven away by the grateful coming of spring and the soft breeze.   Now is the time to wreathe shining heads with myrtle or flowers borne by the freed earth; now is the time in shady groves to make offering to Faunus of a lamb if he ask it, or if he like better, of a kid.   Pale death strikes with impartial foot the huts of poor men and the palaces of kings.   The brief span of life forbids us, happy Sestius, to lay the foundation of a long hope.   (*Carm.* 1. 4. 1-15.)

[3] Lay hold upon to-day, trusting nothing to to-morrow.   (*Carm.* 1. 11. 8.)

be moderate is so often reiterated in his work goes to show that the poet was sincere in giving it. It is no passing fancy, but an integral part of his conduct of life.

Thus we should expect to find Horace a man of simple tastes; and so he professes to be.

> Persicos odi . . . apparatus,[1]

he cries; and though the particular ode is light in tone, the theme is sounded again and again in more serious moments.

> Vile potabis modicis Sabinum
> Cantharis,

he warns no less a person than Maecenas;

> mea nec Falernae
> Temperant vites neque Formiani
> Pocula colles.[2]

> Me pascunt olivae,

he says elsewhere,

> Me cichorea levesque malvae.[3]

Many similar expressions may be found:

> Non ebur neque aureum
> Mea renidet in domo lacunar.
>
> . . . .
> Nihil supra
> Deos lacesso nec potentem amicum
> Largiora flagito,
> Satis beatus unicis Sabinis.[4]

> Purae rivus aquae silvaque iugerum
> Paucorum et segetis certa fides meae
> Fulgentem imperio fertilis Africae
> Fallit sorte beatior.[5]

And so on. A part of this may be, as many scholars would have us believe, a pose; all of it can hardly be.

It naturally follows that Horace is content with his own lot.

> Si natura iuberet,

says he,

[1] I hate the pomp and circumstance of the Persians. (*Carm.* 1. 38. 1.)

[2] You will drink cheap Sabine wine from modest measures. The Falernian vines and the slopes of Formiae do not flavor my cups. (*Carm.* 1. 20. 1-12.)

[3] Olives are my food, and chicory and wholesome mallows. (*Carm.* 1. 31. 15-16.)

[4] Not ivory nor golden ceiling shines resplendent in my house. I ask nothing more of the gods, nor do I importune further my powerful friend, happy enough with just my Sabine farm. (*Carm.* 2. 18. 1-14.)

[5] A stream of pure water and a wood of a few acres and a sure reliance on my crops is a truer happiness than the brilliant lot of the lord of fertile Africa, unconscious of it though he be. (*Carm.* 3. 16. 29-32.)

A certis annis aevum remeare peractum
Atque alios legere, ad fastum quoscumque parentis
Optaret sibi quisque, meis contentus honestos
Fascibus et sellis nollem mihi sumere.[1]

Hoc erat in votis: modus agri non ita magnus,
Hortus ubi et tecto vicinus iugis aquae fons
Et paulum silvae super his foret.　Auctius atque
Di melius fecere.　Bene est.　Nil amplius oro,
Maia nate, nisi ut propria haec mihi munera faxis.[2]

Me . . . .
. . . . . . quid credis, amice, precari?
Sit mihi quod nunc est, etiam minus.[3]

Examples could be multiplied.

From all this we should surmise that Horace was responsive to the charm of external nature; for the person whose tastes are simple rarely fails to admire the beauties which he sees in the undisturbed world about him.　And we cannot deny this habit of mind to the Roman poet.　It is almost impossible to feel that he was insincere in his many protestations of his preference for the country over the town.　The Sabine farm, mentioned so often as his chief treasure, is described in *Epist.* 1. 16 as none but a true lover of nature could describe it.　We see the mountain-range broken only by the dark valley; the oaks and ilex-trees with their grateful shade; the stream (*rivo dare nomen idoneum*), as cool and pure as Hebrus.　The entire picture is given us in a dozen lines, yet it is perfectly distinct.　This, in fact, is the principal merit of the descriptions of external nature in Horace—the creation of a vivid impression by the use of exactly the right word or phrase. What lover of the *Odes* does not know *amoenum Lucretilem* and *Albuneam resonantem* and *praecipitem Anienem?*　We see with Thaliarchus

ut alta stet nive candidum
Soracte;[4]

and the country round about Tibur is familiar ground to us.　What though archaeologists cannot identify all these places?　They are not

---

[1] If nature commanded us to go back from a certain time over our lives again, and to choose whatever other parents each of us would wish for himself according to his pride, I, content with my own, would not want to select new ones honored with state offices. (*Serm.* 1. 6. 93-97.)

[2] This was my prayer: a piece of ground not too large, where there was a garden and a spring of ever-flowing water near the house, and, besides, a little woodland. The gods have done better and more abundantly than this.　It is well.　I ask nothing more, O son of Maia, except that thou make these gifts permanently mine. (*Serm.* 2. 6. 1-5.)

[3] What do you think, my friend, that I pray?　That I may have what now is mine, or even less. (*Epist.* 1. 18. 104-107.)

[4] How Soracte stands white with deep snow. (*Carm.* 1. 9. 1-2.)

the less real to the inward eye of the imagination.

Especially does Horace seem to have delighted in groves and streams. Over and over again he describes himself, or another, stretched at ease beside rippling water, under a shade-giving tree. He nearly always names his trees, and his favorites are many: the arbutus, the ilex, the plane, and the more familiar oak, pine, and poplar. And wherever Horace is known, there also is known the *fons Bandusiae, splendidior vitro.* The poet's promise,

> Fies nobilium tu quoque fontium,
> Me dicente,[1]

has come true.

So marked is this predilection for waters and trees that we are tempted to apply to him his own words:

> Quae Tibur aquae fertile praefluunt,
> Et spissae nemorum comae
> Fingent Aeolio carmine nobilem.[2]

Yet let no one make the mistake of deeming Horace a recluse; for his paramount interest is always *human* nature. He loves the country, but also, notwithstanding temporary periods of distaste, he loves busy Rome with its crowded streets—yes, even with its 'smoke and riches and noise.' His keen eye observes all the people he meets, and his ready mind reproduces them for us, so that we see again the singer Tigellius, and the dinner-giver Nasidienus, and the bore who met him on the Via Sacra, and a host of others, both named and nameless.

Horace was interested not only in the inhabitants of Rome, but in the city itself, then at the height of its glory. Though born in Venusia, he was a true Roman, with all a Roman's pride in the mistress of the world. His patriotism manifests itself in two ways. The first is the obvious one of recounting the triumphs, past and present, of her whom he proudly calls *domina Roma.* We feel that he delights in merely rehearsing the names of the city's great men—

> Romulum . . . an quietem
> Pompili regnum . . . an superbos
> Tarquini fascis . . . an Catonis
> Nobile letum;[3]

---

[1] Thou also shalt become one of the renowned founts through my singing. (*Carm.* 3. 13. 13-14.)

[2] The waters flowing through fertile Tibur and the tangled foliage of the groves shall make him renowned for Aeolian song. (*Carm.* 4. 3. 10-12.)

[3] Romulus, or the peaceful reign of Pompilius, or the proud emblems of Tarquin, or Cato's noble death. (*Carm.* 1. 12. 33-36.)

and in lofty verse he sings the illustrious achievements of the heroes of old:

> Quid debeas, O Roma, Neronibus,
> Testis Metaurum flumen et Hasdrubal
> Devictus et pulcher fugatis
> Ille dies Latio tenebris,
>
> Qui primus alma risit adorea,
> Dirus per urbis Afer ut Italas
> Ceu flamma per taedas vel Eurus
> Per Siculas equitavit undas.
>
> . . . .
>
> Gens quae cremato fortis ab Ilio
> Iactata Tuscis aequoribus sacra
> Natosque maturosque patres
> Pertulit Ausonias ad urbis,
>
> Duris ut ilex tonsa bipennibus
> Nigrae feraci frondis in Algido,
> Per damna, per caedis, ab ipso
> Ducit opes animumque ferro.[1]

Nor do the present glories of Rome less excite his pride. He writes concerning the 'golden age' of Augustus:

> Iam mari terraque manus potentis
> Medus Albanasque timet securis,
> Iam Scythae responsa petunt superbi
> Nuper, et Indi.
>
> Iam Fides et Pax et Honor Pudorque
> Priscus et neglecta redire Virtus
> Audet, adparetque beata pleno
> Copia cornu.[2]

His second method of showing patriotism is very different; for here he appears as the censor, who sees and deplores the evils that threaten his beloved city. The old Roman virtues are no more, he says:

> Di multa neglecti dederunt
> Hesperiae mala luctuosae.

---

[1] What thou owest, O Rome, to the house of Nero the river Metaurus bears witness, and the vanquished Hasdrubal, and the day made beautiful by the driving of darkness from Latium, the first day that smiled with sweet victory since the dread African rode through the cities of Italy as fire goes through pitch-pine or the east wind through the Sicilian waves. The race which bravely bore from the ashes of Ilium to the Ausonian cities its shrines, storm-tossed on Tuscan waters, and its children and old fathers, like an ilex-tree shorn of its branches by cruel axes in Algidus the bearer of dark leaves, draws strength and courage, through losses and wounds, from the sword itself. (*Carm.* 4. 4. 37-60.)

[2] Now on sea and land the Mede fears our powerful bands and our Alban axes; now the Scythians, but lately so arrogant, and the Indians, beg to know our wishes. Now Faith and Peace and Honor and old-time Modesty and neglected Virtue dare to return, and happy Plenty appears with full horn. (*Carm. Saec.* 53-60.)

Iam bis Monaeses et Pacori manus
Non auspicatos contudit impetus
Nostros et adiecisse praedam
Torquibus exiguis renidet.

Paene occupatam seditionibus
Delevit Urbem Dacus et Aethiops.

. . . .

Fecunda culpae saecula nuptias
Primum inquinavere et genus et domos:
Hoc fonte derivata clades
In patriam populumque fluxit.

. . . .

Non his iuventus orta parentibus
Infecit aequor sanguine Punico
Pyrrhumque et ingentem cecidit
Antiochum Hannibalemque dirum.[1]

Not once, but many times, does he sound this note. He foresaw only too well whither the growing luxury and laxity of the empire were tending, and did his best to warn his fellow countrymen. His patriotism, then, was not superficial, but a real part of him, serious and concerned for the future.

The friends of Horace were many, and we may judge from his poems that friendship was no meaningless word to him.

Amicum
Qui non defendit alio culpante, . . .
. . . .
. . . hic niger est, hunc tu, Romane, caveto,[2]

he tells us; and again:

At pater ut gnati, sic nos debemus amici
Siquod sit vitium non fastidire.[3]

His own greatest friend is the powerful minister, Maecenas; and though possibly much of Horace's adulation of him is due to the memory of

[1] The neglected gods have showered many evils upon sorrowful Italy. Already Monaeses and the band of Pacorus have twice crushed our unlucky attacks, and rejoice in having added to their slender necklaces our booty. The Dacian and the Ethiop have nearly destroyed our city racked by rebellion. The age, steeped in guilt, has first polluted wedlock and the race and the home. Calamity, sprung from this source, has overflowed the country and the people. It was not a young manhood born of parents like these that dyed the sea with the blood of Carthage and killed Pyrrhus and great Antiochus and dread Hannibal. (*Carm.* 3. 6. 7-36.)

[2] He who does not defend his friend against another's blame is evil; beware of him, Roman. (*Serm.* 1. 4. 81-85.)

[3] Just as in the case of a father and his son, we ought not to despise a friend because he has some fault. (*Serm.* 1. 3. 43-44.)

benefits conferred, and also to a natural enough pleasure in showing himself to be upon terms of intimacy with so influential a man, we need not deny all sincerity to his protestations of affection for his patron. The beautiful lines,

> Non ego perfidum
> Dixi sacramentum: ibimus, ibimus,
> Utcumque praecedes, supremum
> Carpere iter comites parati,[1]

ring true. And there are humbler friends—humbler, that is, at the time, though nowadays one of them at least is ranked above Augustus himself. This is Virgil, in whose honor Horace wrote his fine *proempticon*, two lines of which serve to express the esteem in which the younger poet held the elder:

> Reddas incolumem precor
> Et serves animae dimidium meae.[2]

Then there are Pompeius, whom our poet addresses as *meorum prime sodalium*, and Septimius, *Gadis aditure mecum*, and a score or more of others, many of them only names to us, but to Horace dear and intimate friends.

No portrait of Horace would be complete without some mention of his delightful sense of humor. It shows itself again and again—now in the description of his brief military experience, now in his account of his meeting with the bore, now in the inimitable bit of dialogue between Lydia and her lover. The humor is generally delicate; yet we cannot use a popular figure and compare it to a rapier-thrust, for it is almost always good-natured. Rarely does Horace approach sarcasm; when he does, it is as likely to be directed against himself as another, for he possesses the happy faculty of laughing at himself.

Here, then, is the Roman poet as he shows himself to us—a genial man and of a kindly disposition, moderate in his life, simple in his tastes, with an artist's eye and feeling for the beauties of external nature, and an artist's interest in humanity; a lover of his country and of his friends; at times giving himself over to mirth and enjoyment, at other times yielding to melancholy; serious withal, and sincerely concerned about what he deemed the great things of life; indeed, a figure to command affection and admiration.

---

[1] I have sworn no false oath: we shall go, whenever you lead the way, we shall go ready to take our last journey as comrades. (*Carm.* 2. 17. 9-12.)

[2] Return him safe, I pray, and preserve the half of my soul. (*Carm.* 1. 3. 7-8.)

When we turn to Horace the artist, we find that all critics, what-

Characteristics of Horace's Poetry. ever may be their feeling about the matter of his poetry, agree that he is a master-craftsman. It is evident to the merest novice that his advice about the use of the file was drawn from his own practice. As a result, whatever he has to say is said in so felicitous a manner as to make us feel it could be altered only for the worse. Especially is this true of the *Odes*, where almost every sentence is an exquisitely cut gem. He has an astonishing power of compression — the faculty of making one or two words imply a dozen ideas. This is what makes it absolutely impossible to translate Horace adequately; yet, by a curious sort of irony, it is perhaps this very perfection that attracts so many would-be translators—men so diverse as Milton and Eugene Field, Cowper and Gladstone. The poet himself evidently realized his own mastery of technique. He speaks of his work as *operosa*.

he boasts;
> Parios ego primus iambos,
>
> Ostendi Latio, numeros animosque secutus
> Archilochi;[1]

and even in the lofty *Exegi monumentum* he rests his chief claim to renown on the fact that he was the first to adapt Aeolian verse to Italian measures.

But, as Horace realizes, and as he more than once tells us, poetry consists not alone in technical skill.

he says,
> Non satis est,
>
> puris versum perscribere verbis,
> Quem si dissolvas, quivis stomachetur eodem
> Quo personatus pacto pater.[2]
>
> Ingenium cui sit, cui mens divinior atque os
> Magna sonaturum, des nominis [poetae] huius honorem.[3]

In his *Satires* and *Epistles*, accordingly, he disclaims the honor:
> Neque, siqui scribat uti nos
> Sermoni propiora, putes hunc esse poetam.[4]

---

[1] I was the first to import Parian iambics into Italy, imitating the numbers and the spirit of Archilochus. (*Epist.* 1. 19. 23-25.)

[2] It is not enough to write a verse in correct language, when if you take it to pieces you find that anybody might storm like the father in the play. (*Serm.* 1. 4. 54-56.)

[3] To him who has genius, to him who has a more godlike mind and a tongue made to speak lofty things, give the honor of this name [poet]. (*Serm.* 1. 4. 43-44.)

[4] If anybody writes, as I do, things more like ordinary talk, don't think he is a poet. (*Serm.* 1. 4. 41-42.)

We prefer to take his valuation of himself in the *Odes:*

> Non omnis moriar. . . . . . .
> . . . . . . Mihi Delphica
> Lauro cinge volens, Melpomene, comam.[1]

The poetry of Horace is far from being the superficial, trivial verse that some critics would have us believe. It is true that he wrote many odes upon conventional themes, treating these themes in such fashion as to make them memorable; it is true that he wrote delicately-finished bits of verse on trifles—*Quis multa gracilis, Persicos odi, Vides ut alta,* and many others; it is also true that he wrote noble poems, such as *Caelo tonantem, Ne forte credas,* and the triumphant *Exegi monumentum,* the first few lines of which are among the finest utterances on the immortality conferred on a poet by his work.

As must be the case with every real artist, Horace rated his calling high. In his opinion, as we have seen (p. 17), the poet must possess *ingenium, mens divinior, os magna sonaturum.* When we find him speaking in a slighting way of poetry, it always proves to be the work of the uninspired, untrained poetaster that he has in mind; for he believed that the poet must be made as well as born. The *Ars Poetica* is a witness to the value he set on his vocation.

> Quod si me lyricis vatibus inseris,

he tells us in a well-known ode,

> Sublimi feriam sidera vertice.[2]

Throughout his works we find evidence of his high esteem for his instrument—perhaps none more satisfying than that in *Carm.* 4. 8:

> Non incisa notis marmora publicis,
> Per quae spiritus et vita redit bonis
> Post mortem ducibus, ...
> . . . . . . clarius indicant
> Laudes quam Calabrae Pierides; neque
> Si chartae sileant quod bene feceris
> Mercedem tuleris.[3]

And for his own writings his prophecy is true: Maecenas the statesman is a shadow; Maecenas the friend and patron of Horace is known to every lover of the poet.

---

[1] I shall not wholly die. Gladly, Melpomene, wreathe my locks with the Delphic laurel. (*Carm.* 3. 30. 6-16.)

[2] But if you rank me with the lyric poets, with my proud head I shall strike the stars. (*Carm.* 1. 1. 35-36.)

[3] Not marbles graven with deeds of public renown, by which breath and life come back to worthy captains after death, show forth praises more clearly than do the Muses of Calabria; and if the written word were stilled you would not bear away the guerdon of what you have done. (*Carm.* 4. 8. 13-22.)

In Horace, then, to borrow the happy phrase of De Quincey, 'the exquisite skill co-operated with the exquisite nature'; and the result is one of the world's treasures. And that the world has treasured his work is abundantly clear. Of all his words none has proved more truly prophetic than

> Postera
> Crescam laude recens. [1]

He has been called the most popular of poets; possibly no other classical writer is so often quoted. This is partly due to the fact that his conciseness makes his verses lend themselves to quotation; yet there is another reason, which is well expressed by Sellar:[2]

'Among all ancient poets he suits the greatest variety of modern tastes. . . . He has an attraction not merely of early association for educated men whose lives are cast in other spheres than that of literature; while to those who seek in the study of great poets to gain some temporary admission within the circle of some of the better thoughts, the finer fancies, the happier and more pathetic experiences of our race, he is able to afford this access. To each successive age or century, he seems to express its own familiar wisdom and experience. . . . He is one of the few ancient writers who unite all the cultivated nations of modern times in a common admiration. They each seem to claim him as especially their own.'

Let it be added that, as has often been noticed, Horace makes an appeal to both young and old. We are told, indeed, that it takes the weight of years to bring a man to a full appreciation of him; for his work, small in quantity though it is, covers his whole life, and he shows us himself at each period, so that there is something for all.

It has been pointed out above (p. 7) that contemporary records of Horace are of the scantiest. That his work was **Horace as seen** admired we may gather from the fact that Augustus **by his Contem-** more than once called his Muse into requisition, **poraries.** and also from the patronage with which Maecenas favored him; but Ovid (*Tristia* 4. 10. 49-50) seems to be the only writer of the times who mentions him:

> Et tenuit nostras numerosus Horatius aures;
> Dum ferit Ausonia carmina culta lyra.[3]

---

[1] In after days I shall ever increase in fame. (*Carm.* 3. 30. 7-8.)

[2] *Horace and the Elegiac Poets*, p. 4.

[3] And tuneful Horace has held our ears, when he strikes well-wrought songs from his Ausonian lyre.

The adjective here applied to the poems of Horace is worthy of note; Ovid evidently appreciated his compatriot's mastery of technique. Yet the praise is mild, and its force is diminished by the fact that Horace is only one in a list of writers mentioned by the other poet, some of them of very doubtful merit. Horace himself, if we may judge at all from his own writings, would seem frequently to imply that he was considered inferior to epic poets such as Virgil, Varius, and Jullus.

> Ego apis Matinae,

he says,

> More modoque
> . . . operosa parvus
> Carmina fingo.[1]

Yet, as the centuries passed, and many of the classic writers **Horace in the** fell into oblivion, Horace was not forgotten. From **Middle Ages.** the ninth century to the thirteenth,[2] every cycle shows a considerable number of Horatian quotations in every important literature; and the Middle Ages produced more than one Horatian specialist such as Conrad von Mure. It was the didactic works of the Roman poet, however, that attracted most attention; the lyrics fell more and more into the background, and in 1280 Hugo of Trimberg wrote:

> Sequitur Horatius, prudens et discretus,
> Vitiorum emulus, firmus et mansuetus;
> Qui tres libros etiam fecit principales,
> Duosque dictaverat minus usuales;
> Epodon videlicet, et librum odarum,
> Quos nostris temporibus credo valere parum.
> Hinc poetrie veteris titulum ponamus,
> Sermones cum epistolis dehinc adiciamus.[3]

Notwithstanding this neglect of what we now consider the flower of his work, Horace was placed upon a lofty pedestal by the men of the Middle Ages. We at once think of Dante's selection of him as one of the five great poets of antiquity, in *Inferno* 4. 89 — where he figures

---

[1] I, after the custom and manner of the Matine bee, fashion in my small way my studied songs. (*Carm.* 4. 2. 27-32.)

[2] A large part of my data for this paragraph comes from Dr. Edward Moore's *Studies in Dante* (first series), pp. 197 ff. This, in turn, derives some of its material from Dr. Manitius' *Analekten zur Geschichte des Horaz im Mittelalter*, which I have consulted.

[3] Next comes Horace, prudent and discreet, jealous of faults, firm and kindly. He wrote three principal books and composed two that are less familiar; namely, a book of epodes and one of odes, which in our times are, I think, of little value. Hence let us set down the title of his *Ancient Poetry* [the *Ars Poetica*], adding also his satires and epistles. (*Registrum Multorum Auctorum*, ll. 66-73.)

as 'Orazio *Satiro.*' Long before this, Alcuin, in the literary circle
which he organized at the court of Charlemagne, assumed the name
of 'Horatius Flaccus.'

When we come nearer home, and regard the first great figure in
English literature, we find only a few traces of Horace
Horace and in Chaucer; and these few, Professor Skeat thinks,
Chaucer. show only a second-hand knowledge.[1] 'It is obvious,'
he says, 'that Chaucer never saw Horace's works in the complete state;
if he had done so, he would have found a writer after his own heart,
and he would have quoted him even more freely than he has quoted
Ovid.' It is worth noting, however, that the few quotations or
paraphrases which we do find are all from the didactic works—a fact
which corroborates the statement made above of the superior popularity of these poems.

But by 'the spacious times of great Elizabeth' the *Odes* had once
more come to their own. We find them trans-
Horace among lated and paraphrased by the poets of the day;
the Elizabethans. quoted by the writers of prose; and even set
down piecemeal in school-books. We remember how Chiron, in *Titus
Andronicus,* says of *Integer vitae:*

> O! 'tis a verse in Horace; I know it well:
> I read it in the grammar long ago.

In fact, most of the Elizabethans must have been familiar with Horace
from early youth. We are told[2] that 'the afternoon lessons of the boys
at Rotherham School [a typical grammar school of the period] in
Shakespeare's time were "two days in Horace, and two days in
Seneca's Tragedies; both which they translated into English." ' Ever
since, let it be added, Horace has served as a text-book for English
schoolboys; thus the fate against which he humorously inveighed has
come upon him:

> Hoc quoque te [meum librum] manet, ut pueros elementa docentem
> Occupet extremis in vicis balba senectus.[3]

That this dislike of having his poems used as texts for schoolboys was
not without reason we shall see when we take up the opinions of several
of the most illustrious of these students; yet there is much to be said
for a system which puts Horace at the end of a man's tongue.

---

[1] *The Works of Geoffrey Chaucer,* ed. Skeat, 2. lii.

[2] J. W. Cunliffe, *The Influence of Seneca on Elizabethan Tragedy,* p. 12.

[3] This also awaits you [my book], that faltering old age shall seize upon you, when in the
suburban schools you shall teach boys their beginner's tasks. (*Epist.* 1. 20. 17-18.)

It is still a question whether the greatest poet among the Elizabethans knew Horace. Since he attended Stratford Grammar School, it is likely that he did; moreover, it seems that his works contain internal evidence of such a knowledge. However that may be, there is no doubt that Ben Jonson was saturated with Horace, even going so far as to call himself by the Roman poet's name in his *Poetaster*; and many other writers of that prolific age show a strong Horatian influence.

As we come down through the cavalier poets, we find the vigorous influence of Horace no whit abated. Herrick, perhaps, echoes him oftener than do any of the others; but all feel his attraction. Milton, as great a contrast to these as could well be imagined, has many reminiscences of Horace. And so it goes until we arrive at the so-called classic period,' when most of the Roman poets were at the high tide of popularity in England, with Horace as one of the leaders.

Horace and the Cavalier Poets.

Horace and Milton.

Throughout the eighteenth century our poet holds his own; when a writer wished to do a bit of elegant translating, or when he stood in need of an apt quotation, more often than not he turned to Horace. But about the beginning of the nineteenth century there was a considerable change in English literature. Poets deliberately turned away from the traditions of the 'classic school,' and began to seek new paths for themselves, or to reopen neglected ones. It might be supposed that Horace, the favorite of the old school, would be discarded by the new; whether or not this was the case, the following pages will attempt to show.

Horace in the Eighteenth Century.

But before separately taking up the great poets of the age, we shall do well to pause for a short time at the two principal divisions of Horace's verse. These have been already referred to as the didactic and the lyric. It remains to see what each group includes, and what influence each has exerted.

Divisions of Horace's Work.

The didactic poems comprise the *Satires*, the *Epistles*, and the *Ars Poetica*. They are all written in dactylic hexameter, and they deal with a variety of subjects in a pleasing conversational way—*sermoni propiora*, as Horace himself puts it. Some are merely narratives of events in the poet's daily life, such as the journey to Brundisium; others rebuke the follies of the time—not after the manner of a Juvenal or a

Swift, but in a gentler way which would correct without stinging. 'Come, let us reason together,' these poems seem to say. 'Let us look impartially at this or that, and see how foolish and harmful it is.' Others treat of philosophy — the poet's philosophy of life, which he has worked out for himself. Some, again, discuss literary matters; many are autobiographical. All are precious, not only for their inherent charm, but as a record of the opinions and actions of a poet; they might almost be entitled, as was *The Prelude* of Wordsworth, 'the growth of a poet's mind.' But to none of them would Horace himself have given the name poetry. As he says in the *Satires*,

> Primum ego me illorum, dederim quibus esse poetas,
> Excerpam numero.[1]

And at the beginning of his first epistle he laments:

> Non eadem est aetas, non mens. . . . . .
> Nunc itaque et versus et cetera ludicra pono.[2]

When we come to the lyrics, however, the case is different. Their bulk is small—four books of *Odes*, one of *Epodes*, and the *Carmen Saeculare*; but, as we have seen, they contain 'songs for man or woman, of all sizes.' They range in tone 'from grave to gay, from lively to severe,' and each style is fittingly handled.

We have already noticed that during the Middle Ages the didactic works of Horace were in the foreground, the lyrics almost forgotten. The Renaissance brought a change; and throughout the latter half of the sixteenth and the first half of the seventeenth century the *Odes* seem to have exerted the greater influence. This was natural; for the poets of those days were in the main essentially singers, caring but little for ethical teachings, and interested in musical language and metres, as well as in the material suitable to lyric treatment. The pendulum swung the other way in the 'classic period,' and the didactic poems came again to the front. The insistence of Horace on polish and finish—an insistence chiefly to be marked in his *Satires* and *Epistles* —could not fail to attract such lovers of elegance as the writers of the age of Anne; his hexameters suited ears which preferred the heroic couplet to any other form of verse. Moreover, Horace was a satirist; and the times were rich in satire, with him as one of the models.

---

[1] I omit myself first of all from the number of those whom I would allow to be poets. (*Serm.* 1. 4. 39-40.)

[2] My age is not the same, nor my mind; so now I lay aside my verses and the rest of my playthings. (*Epist.* 1. 1. 4-10.)

Therefore literary epistles in verse and imitations of Horace—always of the didactic Horace—ran riot, while the *Ars Poetica* was accepted as the gospel of good taste in writing. An age which, with all its merits, was usually so unnatural in its treatment of external nature, and so little interested in the subjectivity which is the essence of the lyric, could hardly be expected fully to appreciate the *Odes* of Horace.

With the return of the subjective to poetry—in the period with which this thesis deals—the lyrics of Horace were once again the most popular part of his work, though the *Satires* and *Epistles* were not forgotten. Even now one occasionally hears an elderly person speak of 'Horace the satirist,' although probably for one reader of the didactic poems there are six of the *Odes*. This is unfortunate: we cannot properly know the poet without seeing him from all sides.

But, in spite of the popularity which Horace has enjoyed among our men of letters, we are perplexed when **With whom may we** we look about for some writer with whom **compare Horace?** to compare him. Is there any one who may claim the honor of being his English analogue? Not Ben Jonson, for all his own confidence in his similarity to the Roman poet whom he so admired. Indeed, we can hardly imagine two great writers temperamentally farther apart than the genial Augustan and the often ungenial Elizabethan. Horace may now and again have been moved to 'strip the ragged follies of the time naked as at their birth,' but his was no 'armed and resolved hand,' no 'whip of steel.' Rather did he believe:

Ridiculum acri
Fortius et melius magnas plerumque secat res.[1]

Points of close resemblance we may find between the nature of Horace as revealed in his writings and the natures of a score or more of authors prominent in our literature. Addison's admirers, moved, we must suppose, by the gentle satire of the *Spectator* papers, have hailed him as the English Horace. Stevenson, perhaps through his inherent Epicureanism, often strongly reminds us of Horace in his *Epistles* and *Satires*. More Horatian than either of these is Thackeray, who, moreover, has so rare a knowledge of the Roman poet as always to be ready, so it seems, with an apt quotation. None of these men, however, can for a moment compare with Horace in his first and preferred capacity— that of writer of lofty and beautiful poetry. We turn to Herrick, who has his supporters; and, indeed, he does at times recall to us the singer

---

[1] Ridicule very often decides things of importance better and more effectually than severity. (*Serm.* 1. 10. 14-15.)

of Lydia and Chloë, Lalage and Leuconoë. But that which is high and serious in Horace—the often neglected side—finds no parallel in Herrick, whose flights are seldom above the roof of his parsonage, despite his own claim that he sings 'of heaven.' Many of our greater poets from time to time remind us of this lofty Horace—the attempt of the following pages will be in part to show this; but none is so near to him as to challenge comparison in all respects.

Is this to say that Horace is greater than any English writer? Not at all: the giants of our literature are as far beyond him as is Homer, and he would be the first to admit it. But, notwithstanding this fact, there is no one who is to English letters what Horace is to Roman— nay, to all—letters. He is unlike all others.

Bearing this in mind, we may now go on to investigate just what sort of influence Horace exerted on each of the foremost poets of the nineteenth century. And the first we meet is Wordsworth, whose *Lyrical Ballads*, published in 1798, mark the beginning of nineteenth-century poetry.

The opinion has somehow become prevalent that Wordsworth as

Wordsworth. a writer was almost uninfluenced by the classics, or, indeed, by any books—that he was a poet largely dependent upon his 'spark of nature's fire.' There could hardly be a greater mistake. Many of the poet's utterances which go to disprove this have been preserved, would people but look for them. One is particularly relevant to the present inquiry: 'First read the ancient classical authors; *then* come to *us*; and you will be able to judge for yourself which of us is worth reading.'[1]

Wordsworth was himself well-read in at least the Roman half of classical literature. The reader of his poems who is also a student of Latin hardly needs the statement which the poet makes in a letter to Walter Savage Landor (April 20, 1822):

'My acquaintance with Virgil, Horace, Lucretius, and Catullus is intimate.'

He adds, indeed, that he 'never read them with a critical view to composition'; but it is certain that their thoughts, and often their language, entered into the texture of his verse, on some occasions, as we shall see, becoming so closely interwoven with his own thought that it is difficult to separate warp from woof.

In the passage just quoted, Horace shares the honors with three great compatriots; but other testimony places him above any of them

---

[1] Christopher Wordsworth, *Memoirs of Wordsworth* 2. 477.

in Wordsworth's favor.   Bishop Wordsworth[1] tells us that his uncle
said:

'How graceful is Horace's modesty in his "Ego *apis* Matinae more
modoque," as contrasted with the Dircaean Swan!   Horace is my
great favorite: I love him dearly.'

Again Wordsworth says, in his *Letter to a Friend of Robert Burns*:

'It is delightful to read what, in the happy exercise of his own
genius, Horace chooses to communicate of himself and his friends.'

We may add to this the evidence of two of Wordsworth's friends.
The Reverend Perceval Graves says of the poet:

'He was a very great admirer of Virgil. . . . From him, and
Horace who was an especial favorite, and Lucretius, he used to quote
much.'[2]

And De Quincey tells us, in his *Literary and Lake Reminiscences*:

'Wordsworth finally became a very sufficient master of the Latin
language, and read certain favorite authors, especially Horace, with a
critical nicety, and with a feeling for the felicities of his composition.'[3]

It is De Quincey, too, who writes, in connection with Coleridge's
Latinity (in *Coleridge and Opium-Eating*):

'It is remarkable that Wordsworth, educated most negligently at
Hawkshead School, subsequently, by reading the lyric poetry of
Horace, simply for his own delight as a student of composition, made
himself a master of Latinity in its most difficult form.'[4]

The reason given for Wordsworth's reading of Horace is evidently a
mistake, since it contradicts the poet's own words; but with regard to
the knowledge itself, De Quincey is doubtless an able judge.

I have been able to find but one dissenting voice on this question,
and that is recorded in a letter from Charles Lloyd the younger to his
father (1809), with reference to the latter's translations of Horace:

'Both Coleridge, Wordsworth, and Southey profess to admire thy
translation of Homer very much, and often voluntarily introduce the
subject in order to express their commendations; but, as a reason for
omitting to obey thy injunction which applies equally to all three, I
must inform thee that I know they have next to a contempt for Horace;
and the best translations that could possibly be conceived of his verses
would not, I believe, give them any pleasure.'

---

[1] *Memoirs of Wordsworth* 2. 479.
[2] See Knight's *Life of Wordsworth* 2. 328.
[3] *Works*, ed. Masson, 2. 265.
[4] *Works*, ed. Masson, 5. 204.

Lloyd then goes on to enumerate particular reasons for his not showing the translations to the three in question. Wordsworth 'is so much occupied . . . with a pamphlet which he has in the press on the Portuguese Convention'; Coleridge is 'miserable in mind and body'; Southey has 'an invincible dislike to Horace.' Of him alone is this said individually; and when we recall that Wordsworth's pamphlet bears on its title-page a long quotation from Horace, we are not inclined to attach great importance to Lloyd's inclusive statement.

But what in Horace especially appeals to Wordsworth? Why should the later poet speak of the earlier as 'my great favorite'? The full appreciation of poetry must be based upon a sympathy existing between author and reader. It remains to discover wherein lies this sympathy between the Roman and the English bards.

Wordsworth himself gives us the key to his preference when, in praising Horace, he speaks of his 'graceful modesty,' and of 'what he chooses to communicate of himself and his friends.' A further testimony is found in the poem called *Liberty* (ll. 96-110):

> Let easy mirth his social hours inspire,
> And fiction animate his sportive lyre,
> Attuned to verse that, crowning light Distress,
> With garlands, cheats her into happiness;
> Give *me* the humblest note of those sad strains
> Drawn forth by pressure of his gilded chains,
> As a chance-sunbeam from his memory fell
> Upon the Sabine farm he loved so well;
> Or when the prattle of Bandusia's spring
> Haunted his ear—he only listening—
> He proud to please, above all rivals, fit
> To win the palm of gaiety and wit;
> He, doubt not, with involuntary dread,
> Shrinking from each new favor to be shed,
> By the world's Ruler, on his honored head!

Here, then, is the Horace whom Wordsworth 'loved dearly'—not the humorist, nor the singer who strove to forget or cover up gloomy thoughts; not particularly, it would seem, the patriot deeply concerned for his country's welfare, nor the apostle of moderation and contentment, though in both interests the Roman poet and Wordsworth had much in common; but, above all, the lover of external nature, the bard who modestly considered his genius *tenuis grandia*, the conversational recorder of little daily happenings. Horace resting at ease beneath ilex or arbutus, listening to 'the prattle of Bandusia's spring' and resolving to immortalize it, or Horace watching the sun fall below the 'continuous mountains' which protected his farm, would have a peculiar attraction for the poet who sympathetically scrutinized celandine and daffodil, cuckoo and green linnet; and Horace spending a pleasant evening by his modest fireside, while out of doors the snow fell so deep that *nec iam sustineant onus silvae laborantes*, must seem near akin to the man who loved to sit

> In the loved presence of my cottage-fire,
> And listen to the flapping of the flame,
> Or kettle whispering its faint undersong.

One who says of himself,

> The moving accident is not my trade;
> To freeze the blood I have no ready arts:
> 'Tis my delight, alone in summer shade,
> To pipe a simple song for thinking hearts,

would be sure to admire the 'graceful modesty' of Horace as shown in the famous passage about the 'Matine bee,' and elsewhere. And above all, the things that Horace 'chooses to communicate of himself and his friends' would be appreciated by one who knew so well as Wordsworth the value of companionable friendship. This aspect of the English poet is often neglected; but we have only to read the letters of the Wordsworth family to realize that the circle of acquaintances which had its centre at Grasmere was held to this centre by ties unusually close. Just as Horace had for friends Maecenas, Virgil, Aristius Fuscus, so Wordsworth had the Beaumonts, Coleridge, Henry Crabb Robinson, and others. Moreover, the man who could write *The Prelude*, as well as other autobiographical poems (for Wordsworth also is very self-revealing), could not fail to enjoy the confidences of Horace about himself.

In view of all this, it is not surprising that we find Wordsworth the most Horatian of all the poets considered in this study. Others may quote more frequently; but it is he who appears most thoroughly to have assimilated the spirit of Horace. At times he seems actually to reproduce that spirit — or rather, the part of it which he especially admired.

Very different is the case of Wordsworth's fellow-poet and friend, **Coleridge.** Coleridge. De Quincey points out (and doubtless truly enough, since his testimony is corroborated by what we know of the training afforded by Christ's Hospital) that the early linguistic studies of Coleridge were necessarily thorough and far-reaching; but he goes on to say:[1]

'Latin, from his regular scholastic training, naturally he read with a scholar's fluency; and indeed he read constantly in authors such as Petrarch, Erasmus, Calvin, etc., whose *prose* works he could not then have found in translations. But Coleridge had not cultivated an acquaintance with the delicacies of classic Latinity.'

In Coleridge's own high praise of his schoolmaster, the Reverend James Boyer, he makes no mention of having studied Horace at Christ's Hospital, save for an inclusive 'those [poets] of the Augustan era'; and indeed his only reference, so far as I have been able to discover, to his having used our poet as a text-book occurs in a letter, written to his brother from Cambridge (January 24, 1792), regarding a scholarship examination:

'The examination for my year is "the last book of Homer, and Horace's *De Arte Poetica*." '

Evidently any early acquaintance with Horace which he might have had made no deep impression on his mind, although three early poems—*Easter Holidays*, *Dura Navis*, and *Nil Pejus est Caelibe Vita*, all written in 1787—show traces of Horatian influence. But neither then nor later do we find evidence of any real fondness; in *Table Talk*, collected by Coleridge's nephew during the last years of the poet's life, virtually every well-known Latin author except Horace is discussed.

There are, however, in Coleridge's prose writings a few expressions of admiration for this poet. The most enthusiastic is from *A Lay Sermon*:

'I will refer you to the darling of the polished court of Augustus, to the man whose works have been in all ages deemed the models of good sense, and are still the pocket companions of those who pride themselves on uniting the scholar with the gentleman. This accomplished man of the world has given an account of the subjects of conversation between the illustrious statesmen who governed and the brightest luminaries who then adorned the empire of the civilized world.'[2]

The quotation from the *Satires* which follows leaves no room for doubt as to who is meant by 'this accomplished man of the world.' As for the qualities which Coleridge praises in Horace, they are the very ones which Wordsworth tells us did not appeal to him. Yet, generous as this praise is, there is something about it that does not

---

[1] *Coleridge and Opium-Eating, Works*, ed. Masson, 5. 204.

[2] *Works*, ed. Shedd, 1. 435-436.

ring true. It is as if the writer accepted the fact of Horace's excel-
lence because it had been agreed upon by 'all ages,' but at the same
time did not himself feel any of the things he was saying.

More spontaneous is a sentence from a letter to Thomas Poole
(January 28, 1810):

'Read, for instance, Milton's prose tracts, and only *try* to conceive
them translated into the style of *The Spectator*, or the finest part of
Wordsworth's pamphlet. It would be less absurd to wish that the
serious *Odes* of Horace had been written in the same style as his
Satires and *Epistles.*'

We see from this that Coleridge realized that Horace had written
serious poems—a fact which, as we know, many readers miss; and the
implication is that he admired them, and considered their style suited
to their subjects.

Again, we find Horace mentioned in Coleridge's notes on Luther's
Table Talk:

' "Fulgentius [says Luther] is the best poet, and far above Horace
both with sentences, fair speeches, and good actions; he is well worthy
to be ranked and numbered with and among the poets."

'*Der Teufel!* Surely the epithets should be reversed. . . .
The *super*-Horatian effulgence of Master Foolgentius! O Swan! thy
critical cygnets are but goslings.'[1]

In criticizing Wordsworth's theory of poetic diction, Coleridge
writes with reference to irrelevant particularization in composition:

'Nothing but biography can justify this. If it be admissible even
in a *novel*, it must be one in the manner of De Foe's, that were meant to
pass for histories, not in the manner of Fielding's. . . . Much
less, then, can it be legitimately introduced in a *poem*, the characters of
which, amid the strongest individualization, must still remain repre-
sentative. The precepts of Horace on this point are grounded on the
nature both of poetry and of the human mind. They are not more
peremptory than wise and prudent.'[2]

This raises an interesting point. Coleridge the poet, as we shall
further observe, seems not to have been particularly drawn to Horace
the poet; but Coleridge the literary critic would not fail to be im-
pressed by the value of Horace's criticism. This is also shown by
another quotation from the *Biographia Literaria*:

'But it was as little objected by others as dreamt of by the poet

---

[1] *Works*, ed. Shedd, 5. 298.
[2] *Biographia Literaria*, ed. Shawcross, 2.106-107.

[Southey] himself that he *preferred* careless and prosaic lines on rule and of forethought, or indeed that he pretended to any other art or theory of poetic diction besides that which we may all learn from Horace, Quintilian, the admirable dialogue *De Causis Corruptae Eloquentiae*, or Strada's *Prolusions.*'[1]

Here, then, is all the direct testimony that we have about Coleridge's feeling for Horace; for we can attach no importance to the statement of Charles Lloyd (see p. 26). When we turn to the indirect evidence afforded by the traces of Horace discernible in Coleridge's writings, two points are at once noticeable. First, these traces are nearly all quotations, and for the most part are found in the prose writings. Now Coleridge, like other Englishmen educated in public schools, liked to scatter fragments of Latin throughout his prose; and all the important Roman authors were grist for his mill. The second point is a corollary of the first: the influence of Horace on Coleridge's poetry is almost negligible. This is more truly the case with him than with any other poet we shall study, Keats alone excepted. It is not that Coleridge did not know Horace, but simply that he was not affected by him. The two men, in the capacity of poet, are utterly unlike. Coleridge, with his taste for the intricacies of German metaphysics, could hardly agree with Horace's Epicurean philosophy and his precepts for right living; and Coleridge's subjects for poetry are not those of Horace. Who can imagine the latter treating such material as that of *Christabel* or *The Rime of the Ancient Mariner?* Temperamentally the two were different; and accordingly the one did not to any appreciable extent react on the other. To Coleridge, Horace was 'the darling of the polished court of Augustus,' and little more.

Byron. When we turn to Byron, we find that most of those who know anything of his opinions about Horace know them by only one line:

> Then farewell, Horace—whom I hated so.[1]

Thus the poet receives an undeserved reputation for absolute scorn of Horace—a reputation which would never be his if his detractors would read no more than the context of the line. I quote here the three stanzas which contain the complete thought:

> These hills seem things of lesser dignity;
> All, save the lone Soracte's height, displayed

[1] *Biographia Literaria*, ed. Shawcross, 1. 40.
[2] *Childe Harold's Pilgrimage* 4. 77.

Not *now* in snow, which asks the lyric Roman's aid
  For our remembrance, and from out the plain
  Heaves like a long-swept wave about to break,
  And on the curl hangs pausing: not in vain
  May he who will his recollections rake,
  And quote in classic raptures, and awake
  The hills with Latin echoes—I abhorred
  Too much to conquer for the Poet's sake
  The drilled dull lesson, forced down word by word
In my repugnant youth, with pleasure to record

  Aught that recalls the daily drug which turned
  My sickening memory; and, though Time hath taught
  My mind to meditate what then it learned,
  Yet such the fixed inveteracy wrought
  By the impatience of my early thought,
  That, with the freshness wearing out before
  My mind could relish what it might have sought,
  If free to choose, I cannot now restore
Its health—but what it then detested, still abhor.

  Then farewell, Horace—whom I hated so,
  Not for thy faults, but mine: it is a curse
  To understand, not feel thy lyric flow,
  To comprehend, but never love thy verse;
  Although no deeper Moralist rehearse
  Our little life, nor Bard prescribe his art,
  Nor livelier Satirist the conscience pierce,
  Awakening without wounding the touched heart,
Yet fare thee well—upon Soracte's ridge we part.

This serves to explain any positive dislike that Byron manifests
for Horace; it lies rooted in the memory of school-days, when studying
Latin was a required task. Years afterward we find Tennyson making the same complaint; but Tennyson outgrew his distaste, while
Byron, it would seem, never did. Moore says:

'It was not till released from the duty of reading Virgil as a task
that Gray could feel himself capable of enjoying the beauties of that
poet; and Lord Byron was, to the last, unable to vanquish a similar
prepossession with which the same sort of school association had
inoculated him against Horace.'[1]

Yet it is dangerous to accept the statement without qualifica-
tion. It is never safe to judge a man on partial evidence; and it is
doubly unsafe in the case of Byron, who wrote impulsively, and
whose opinions were so changeful that after reading his most positive

[1] *Life of Byron* 1. 98

assertions we find ourselves asking: 'Will he have the same feeling the next day?' To take a single instance, we find him writing to Murray, after the publication of Keats' *Hyperion*:

'Here are [*sic*] Johnny Keats' . . . poetry. . . . Pray send me *no more* poetry but what is rare and decidedly good. There is such a trash of Keats and the like upon my tables that I am ashamed to look at them. . . . No more Keats, I entreat:—flay him alive; if you don't, I must skin him myself: there is no bearing the drivelling idiotism of the Manikin.'

A year later he writes:

'My indignation at Mr. Keats' depreciation of Pope has hardly permitted me to do justice to his own genius, which, *malgré* all the fantastic fopperies of his style, was undoubtedly of great promise. His fragment of *Hyperion* seems actually inspired by the Titans, and is as sublime as Aeschylus. He is a loss to our literature.'

Nevertheless, though it is difficult to say anything definite about the opinions of a man who was so unstable, it is probably true that Byron never greatly cared for Horace, and this despite the fact that he quotes him copiously. As we have seen, the English poet was forced into a close acquaintance with Latin at Harrow; and that 'almost preternatural' memory of his, of which Mary Shelley speaks, permanently recorded these early impressions, though often, let us add, inexactly. It is not strange, then, that we find him writing on the fly-leaf of his *Scriptores Graeci*,[1] where were inscribed the names of some old friends at school:

> Eheu fugaces, Postume, Postume,
> Labuntur anni;

and he scattered phrases from Horace through his correspondence. Occasionally he gives the reference for his quotation, showing that he did not always disdain verifying, despite his youthful vaunt in his *List of Historical Writers whose Works I Have Perused in Different Languages* (1807): 'Greek and Latin without number;—these last I shall give up in future.'[2]

Notwithstanding these frequent quotations, Byrons seems always to speak of Horace in a rather patronizing manner. 'The great little poet,' he calls him in *Don Juan* (14. 77); and in spite of the regret ex-

---

[1] See Moore's *Life of Byron* 1. 91.

[2] Moore, *Life of Byron* 1. 143.

pressed in the passage from *Childe Harold* (above, pp. 31-32), we cannot help feeling that the 'curse' is one to which Byron willingly submits, indeed taking some pride in his idiosyncrasy. The 'lyric flow' of Horace he never attains, even at his best, and therefore it was inevitable, considering the kind of man he was, that he should underrate it. It is characteristic of Byron to be careless in his use of language, both as regards sound and sense. He wrote easily and rapidly — *in hora saepe ducentos versus dictabat stans pede in uno*, as Horace says of Lucilius; and he could not appreciate the exquisite skill and pains with which the other molded his verse. He would rather scorn such care for detail; and although he could paraphrase the *Ars Poetica*, he could not benefit by all its precepts.

All this bears upon Horace as a lyric poet. When we come to the second division of his work, there is another story to tell. It is significant that the praise given in *Childe Harold* is to Horace the 'moralist,' the 'satirist,' and the 'prescriber of his art.' In other words, Byron cared most for the *Epistles*, the *Satires*, and the *Ars Poetica*.

Byron himself was a satirist of extraordinary power. *Don Juan*, generally conceded to be his greatest work, is mainly satirical; and many of his other poems belong to this *genre*. We are at once led to ask whether these satires show the spirit of Horace—that spirit which, as we have seen, preferred argument to invective. But the answer to such a question must be negative. Byron could comment admiringly on Horace's power of 'awakening without wounding the touched heart'; but when he himself came to deal with the things in the universe to which he objected, he was usually as savage as Juvenal or Persius. Either he adopted a cynical attitude towards the follies of mankind, or he loosed himself from all restraint, and launched forth into bitterness which a century after makes us wince. Horace nearly always refers to the poets of his time with great generosity, and when he finds fault does it without leaving a sting; we cannot imagine him uttering the insults which Byron heaped upon Wordsworth, upon Keats, and above all upon Southey—but indeed, upon almost all contemporary men of letters.

We now come to the closest approach of Byron to Horace—the *Hints from Horace*, a paraphrase of the *Ars Poetica*. Byron took a greater interest in this than in any of his other works. 'I look upon it and my Pulci as by far the best things of my doing,' he writes to Murray in 1821, ten years after making the paraphrase; and he shows unwonted eagerness about the proof-sheets of it. Moore, too, mentions this 'preference of the Horatian Paraphrase.'[1]

It seems strange enough that so negligent an artist as Byron should choose to work with a theory of poetry; but it becomes less strange when we read the *Hints*. In the precepts for writing, Byron in general merely translates Horace, making good his boast, found in a letter to Murray, of his fidelity to the original. He substitutes names, but not ideas; he is simply transcribing precepts which he himself usually honors in the breach. But frequently he uses the Horatian maxims to introduce digressions of his own, and these are pure Byronic satire. The interpolations constitute a large part of the poem, and make it rather a piece of bitter satirical verse than an epistle about literature, with only an incidental element of mild satire, as is the original. The *Hints from Horace*, therefore, so far from being really Horatian in tone, rather serves to accentuate Byron's lack of sympathy with Horace.

That, indeed, there was a lack we cannot doubt. Byron knew Horace widely, but superficially. He never realized the true value of the Roman poet in the world's literature. He was proud of paraphrasing the *Ars Poetica*, because he considered it 'the most difficult poem in the language';[2] but he looked upon it rather as a vehicle for personal satire than a treatise to be studied and followed. And aside from it and an indifferent early translation of part of the famous ode *Iustum et tenacem*, the many traces of Horace found in his poems are nearly all chance phrases, quoted either in Latin or in English. They are, on the whole, external embellishments, not real elements of the poet's work; in perhaps every case they are consciously and deliberately used. We cannot refuse to believe Byron when he tells us that he could never love the verse of Horace; we may doubt the other part of the statement—that he comprehended it, in the sense in which he uses the word. Yet, as I have tried to show, we are mistaken if we take the 'hated so' as literal and abiding.

If we should attempt — and the attempt has been made — to divide English poets into two classes, calling one class
Shelley.
Greeks, and the other Romans, according to their characteristics and the influences to which they have responded, we should unhesitatingly put Byron among the Romans; and just as unhesitatingly we should place the poet whose name is oftenest asso-

---

[1] *Life of Byron* 2. 18.
[2] See letter to R. C. Dallas, September 4, 1811.

ciated with his—Shelley—with the Greeks. Nor should we make a mistake in this: Shelley's work is decidedly more Greek than Latin, and to him the literature and ideals of Greece meant more than those of any other nation. 'You see how ill I follow the maxim of Horace,' he writes to Thomas Love Peacock (January 26, 1819), 'at least in its literal sense: *nil admirari* — which I should say, *prope res est una* — to prevent there ever being anything admirable in the world.' And then rashly, 'Fortunately Plato is of my opinion; and I had rather err with Plato than be right with Horace.' And in the preface to *Hellas* he says:

'We are all Greeks. Our laws, our literature, our religion, our arts have their root in Greece. But for Greece, Rome, the instructor, the conqueror, or the metropolis of our ancestors, would have spread no illumination with her arms, and we might still have been savages and idolaters.'

Yet we must not forget that Shelley for a great part, if not all, of his life knew Latin much better than Greek, and that his early training, like that of all Englishmen educated in the public schools of his day, placed far greater emphasis on the language and literature of the Romans. We are told that early in his married life, 'whilst reading Greek classics with the help of "cribs," he [was] teaching Harriet Latin so as to give her a general notion of Horace's *Odes* and Ovid's *Metamorphoses*.'[1] And though he later became so expert in Greek as to make many fine translations, he never forgot Latin in his preference for the other tongue. He writes in the preface to *The Revolt of Islam*:

'The poetry of ancient Greece and Rome and modern Italy and our own country has been to me, like external nature, a passion and an enjoyment.'

That he knew Horace well there is abundant evidence; and we also learn that his acquaintance with the Roman poet was not confined to his school-days. We have already seen that he read the *Odes* with Harriet. In later years Horace appears in the list of books which were at once his study and pleasure, along with Aeschylus, Aristophanes, Theocritus, Xenophon, Herodotus, Lucian, and Virgil.[2] It is true that he never ranks Horace with the great names of Greek literature; in the *Defense of Poetry* he says that 'Horace, Catullus, Ovid, and generally the other great writers of the Virgilian age saw man and nature

---

[1] Jeaffreson, *The Real Shelley* 2. 140.

[2] See Dowden, *Life of Shelley* 2. 215.

in the mirror of Greece.' Yet that he does give him a high place in literature is implied by a paragraph in the preface to *Prometheus Unbound*:

'Poets . . . are, in one sense, the creators, and, in another, the creations, of their age. From this subjection the loftiest do not escape. There is a similarity between Homer and Hesiod, between Aeschylus and Euripides, between Virgil and Horace, between Dante and Petrarch, between Shakespeare and Fletcher, between Dryden and Pope.'

And again, in the *Defense of Poetry*:

'Let us for a moment stoop to the arbitration of popular breath, and . . . let us decide without trial, testimony, or form, that certain of those who are "there sitting where we dare not soar" are reprehensible. Let us assume that Homer was a drunkard, that Virgil was a flatterer, that Horace was a coward. . . . Posterity has done ample justice to the great names now referred to.'

This placing of Horace among the greatest men in literature is doing him greater justice than ever came from Byron or Coleridge. Indeed, it was inevitable that Shelley, with his wonderful lyric gift, should appreciate the felicity of expression, the melody of language and cadence, of his Roman predecessor. It is noteworthy that he always considers Horace in the capacity of lyric poet. In the preface to *The Revolt of Islam* he says:

'Poetry and the art which professes to regulate and limit its powers cannot subsist together. Longinus could not have been the contemporary of Homer, nor Boileau of Horace.'

He here deliberately disregards Horace as a literary critic, although on occasion he quotes the *Ars Poetica*. Most of his citations, however, are from the *Odes*; and in nearly every echo of Horace other than quotation which we find in Shelley's works the influence comes from the lyric poetry. It is unnecessary to remark that to such echoes we must look for a real accord between two poets. Quotation is a more or less artificial thing; we all quote the writers with whom we happen to be most familiar, rather than those for whom we care most —though often, of course, the two classes coincide. But when one poet incorporates the thoughts or expressions of another into his own work, making them a part of himself, so to speak, we may be sure that the two possess some bond of fellowship.

Now this is just what Shelley does, to a limited extent, with the

lyrics of Horace. Fundamentally the two men were very different.
Shelley would never, after fighting on the side of Brutus at Philippi,
have settled down in Rome and enjoyed the patronage of Augustus;
Horace would never have attempted to excite the Irish by throwing
handbills out of the windows to them.   Horace was naturally an Epicurean; Shelley was steeped in Platonic and neo-Platonic doctrines.
But since both were lyric poets, Shelley could appreciate Horace's gift
of expression. He probably could not appreciate it so fully as could a
more careful artist like Tennyson; but his poetic feeling showed him
something of its beauty, and to that extent he was influenced by
Horace more truly than was the case with Byron.

The traces of Horace in the works of Keats are so slight as to be
Keats.   virtually negligible.   In the entire body of his poetry I have
been able to find no certain proof of an acquaintance with
the Roman poet; and the two or three chance phrases in his letters
might have been picked up from various sources.   Fortunately there
is a sentence from a letter to John Hamilton Reynolds (February, 1820)
which proves that Keats had read for himself at least a part of Horace:

'If I were well enough, I would paraphrase an ode of Horace's for
you, on your embarking in the seventy years ago style.   The packet
will bear a comparison with a Roman galley, at any rate.'

This paraphrase of Horace's *proempticon* was probably never made;
but the reference to the ode (1. 3) shows that Keats knew it.   Whether
he, like most of the other poets included in the present study, made his
first acquaintance with Horace in his school-days is doubtful, for his
early education was not thorough.   It is probable that he never
read Latin with much ease.   'When I have done this language [Italian]
so as to be able to read it tolerably well,' he writes to his brother George
in September, 1819, 'I shall set myself to get complete in Latin, and
there my learning must stop.   .   .   .   I would not go so far if I were
not persuaded of the power the language gives me.'   It was his life
which stopped rather than his learning, and he probably was unable to
carry out his intention of 'getting complete' in Latin.   Yet among the
books that he left was a copy of *Auctores Mythographi Latini* which
showed signs of having been used—and in one place, at least, misunderstood.[1]

But we cannot ascribe Keats' freedom from Horatian influence
altogether to his incomplete knowledge of Latin; for, although he

[1] Starick. *Die Belesenheit von John Keats*, p. 70.

knew no Greek at all, his work was greatly influenced by translations from that language. As truly as Shelley, though in a different way, he was a 'Greek'; perhaps this is one reason why Latin literature did not especially attract him. 'I have loved the principle of beauty in all things,' he wrote to Fanny Brawne—a sentence which manifests the Hellenic spirit as we now regard it. It is the principle on which all his best poetry is founded, and it is not distinctively Roman.

Then, too, Keats consciously endeavored to avoid foreign influence. To his brother George he wrote (September, 1819):

'I shall never become attached to a foreign idiom so as to put it into my writings. The *Paradise Lost*, though so fine in itself, is a corruption of our language. . . . Miltonic verse cannot be written, but is the verse of art. I wish to devote myself to another verse alone.'

It is idle to speculate whether Keats would have outgrown these youthful notions—whether he would really have perfected himself in Latin, and thus have come to a fuller appreciation of the worth of its literature. The time he longed for was denied him; he died, leaving work of great value and of still greater promise.

We may say, then, that Keats' knowledge of Latin was probably insufficient to let him appreciate the quality in Horace that attracted Shelley—beautiful diction and rhythm; and that, for the rest, Keats was too remote in temperament from the other to enjoy him greatly. The things he cared for were not those for which Horace cared; hence we find no Horatian element in his poetry.

Tennyson. In 1850, when Wordsworth died, the last as well as the first of that generation of poets, the office of Poet Laureate was conferred upon Tennyson; and by an interesting coincidence, the second Laureate among our seven poets stands immediately after the first in point of the influence exerted upon him by Horace.

There are several reasons for this. In the first place, Tennyson received the customary classical education of the sons of English gentlemen, but, unlike many boys so educated, responded well to it, so that his works show a wide knowledge of all the great Latin poets. It is significant that the author in whom he was most thoroughly grounded in his boyhood was Horace. Then, too, among all English writers none is more careful in the use of his medium than Tennyson. He worked over his verses with the care of a scholar joined to the sensibility of an artist, always striving for felicity of expression and beauty of diction; he suppressed poems when he came to feel that they did not do him justice, until one can hardly make sure that one has studied the entire body even of his published work. It was inevitable that so painstaking a workman should admire the skill of the greatest Latin master of poetical technique; indeed, we shall find him frequently expressing his admiration for the art of Horace. Furthermore, the two poets have many characteristics in common. Though Tennyson's philosophy of life is loftier than that of Horace, he, too, believes in moderation and simplicity. He, too, loved external nature — not, as did Keats, for its sheer sensuous beauty, nor as did Shelley, for the spirit which he felt to be incorporated in it, but rather as did Horace, and, usually, Wordsworth — for the calm comfort and enjoyment which he received from it. And he, too, shows in his poetry a vein of melancholy, which is not relieved, however, by so genial a strain of humor as is the Roman poet's.

Tennyson's first acquaintance with Horace did not promise any great future liking. 'My father,' writes Hallam Tennyson, 'said that he himself received a good but not a regular classical education. At any rate he became an accurate scholar, the author "thoroughly drummed" into him being Horace; whom he disliked in proportion. He would lament: "They use *me* as a lesson-book at schools, and they will call me 'that horrible Tennyson.' It was not till many years after boyhood that I could like Horace. Byron expressed what I felt: 'Then farewell, Horace, whom I hated so.' Indeed I was so overdosed with Horace that I hardly do him justice even now that I am old." '[1]

If it was an overdose, it nevertheless was productive of good results, as the event showed. Had we only this single expression from Tennyson about Horace, we should know that he came to appreciate the Latin poet. For a man's words, which are but the record of passing moods, are not of so much account as his actions; and no student of Horace can read Tennyson without realizing that the later poet cared much for the earlier.

That his fondness, however, came comparatively late in life is again made clear by his son, who quotes the poet as saying:

' "X— has said that Tennyson told him that Horace and Keats were his two masters. X— must have misunderstood," ' and adds: 'He did not care for Horace at all until after he was thirty. He had

---

[1] Hallam Tennyson, *Alfred Lord Tennyson* 1. 16.

said "Horace and Keats are masters." " '[1]

William Allingham corroborates this. He tells us that Tennyson said to him: 'I never appreciated Horace until I was forty.'[2]

There is abundant evidence of Tennyson's admiration of some of Horace's metres. Palgrave, in his recollections of Tennyson, records that 'he [was] deeply moved by the Roman dignity which Horace has imparted to the Sapphic in the *Non enim gazae*; . . . although,' he adds, 'in general Tennyson did not admire the Horatian treatment of that metre, which he would audaciously define, alluding to the Adonic fourth line, as "like a pig with its tail tightly curled." '[3]

But for the Alcaics of Horace he has only praise. In his own note to *The Daisy* he says: 'In a metre which I invented, representing in some measure the grandest of metres, the Horatian Alcaic.' His son also refers to this: 'He was proud of the metre of *The Daisy*, which he called a far-off echo of the Horatian Alcaic.'[4]

The poet makes the following note to his own *Alcaics*:

'My Alcaics are not intended for Horatian Alcaics, nor are Horace's Alcaics the Greek Alcaics, nor are his Sapphics, which are vastly inferior to Sappho's, the Greek Sapphics. The Horatian Alcaic is perhaps the stateliest metre in the world except the Virgilian hexameter at its best. . . . I did once begin an Horatian Alcaic Ode to a great painter, of which I only recollect one line:

Munificently rewarded Artist.'

Hallam Tennyson, in his journal for March 17, 1890, writes of his father:

'He had all but recovered from his influenza, and sat in the sun in front of the study window, and read Jebb's *Homer;* quoted *Virtus repulsae nescia sordidae*, and dwelt on the stateliness imparted by Horace to the Alcaic stanza.'[5]

This quoting from Horace in conversation would seem to have been no infrequent thing. For instance, Hallam Tennyson notes (April 10, 1892):

'My father and Warren walked in the ball-room. My father

[1] Hallam Tennyson, *Alfred Lord Tennyson* 2. 386.

[2] Allingham and Radford, *William Allingham: a Diary*, p. 350.

[3] *Alfred Lord Tennyson* 2. 500.

[4] *Ibid.* 2. 341.

[5] *Ibid.* 2. 377.

quoted the line of Horace,

Nec satis est pulchra esse poemata, dulcia sunto,

and asked Warren to explain it.' [1]

It is evident that Tennyson's early and thorough grounding in
Horace did not give him, in his own opinion, a sufficient knowledge
to last through life; for Hallam Tennyson says, in describing the
journey to Italy in 1851:

'He took with him his usual traveling companions, Shakespeare,
Milton, Homer, Virgil, Horace, Pindar, Theocritus, and probably the
Divina Commedia and Goethe's *Gedichte.*' [2]

Truly an illustrious group of travelers! It is pleasant to fancy
Tennyson reading Horace on the soil of that Italy dearer to the Latin
poet than

claram Rhodon aut Mytilenen
Aut Epheson bimarisve Corinthi
Moenia vel Baccho Thebas vel Apolline Delphos
Insignis aut Thessala Tempe.[3]

Nor did Tennyson's early training cause him to refrain from teaching Horace to his own sons while they were children. 'The first Latin
I learnt from him,' writes his son Hallam, 'was Horace's *O fons Bandusiae.*' [4]

There are other witnesses to Tennyson's admiration for Horace.
Allingham says that Tennyson remarked to him: 'Catullus, Horace,
and the others gave only their best.' [5]

In Palgrave's personal recollections of Tennyson we read: 'Much
as he loved Horace, he rose above the epigrammatic narrowness of his
brilliant *Non di, non homines.*' [6]

And Palgrave records another allusion to Horace by the poet:

' "The poet's work is his life, and no one has a right to ask for
more," he would always say; reaching once even the barbarity, as I
could not help calling it, that if Horace had left an autobiography, and
the single manuscript were in his hands, he would throw it into the
fire.' [7]

---

[1] *Alfred Lord Tennyson* 2. 403.

[2] *Ibid.* 1. 341.

[3] Far-famed Rhodes, or Mytilene, or Ephesus, or the walls of Corinth with its two seas, or Thebes
renowned for Bacchus, or Delphi for Apollo, or Thessalian Tempe. (*Carm.* 1. 7. 1-4.)

[4] *Alfred Lord Tennyson* 1. 370.

[5] Allingham and Radford, *William Allingham: a Diary,* p. 294.

[6] Hallam Tennyson, *Alfred Lord Tennyson* 2. 506.

[7] *Ibid.* 2. 484.

This, let us observe, is different from the well-known attitude of Browning. The latter discountenances any expectation by the public that a poet will reveal his own personality through his works; Tennyson's objection is to inquiries about the poet *outside* of his works. But that his objection was not absolute is proved by his having consented to the writing of his memoir by his son.

We must now observe an utterance of Tennyson which would seem at first thought to be in opposition to an inquiry like the present. The poet says, in his introductory notes to *The Princess:*

'There is, I fear, a prosaic set growing up among us, editors of booklets, book-worms, index-hunters, or men of great memories and no imagination, who *impute themselves* to the poet, and so believe that *he*, too, has no imagination, but is for ever poking his nose between the pages of some old volume in order to see what he can appropriate. They will not allow one . . . even to use such a simple expression as the ocean "roars," without finding out the precise verse in Homer or Horace from which we have plagiarized it.'

The same example is given by Hallam Tennyson:

'He himself had been "most absurdly accused of plagiarizing," e.g., "The moanings of the homeless sea," "moanings" from Horace, "homeless" from Shelley. "As if no one else had heard the sea moan except Horace." '[1]

Evidently this particular charge had made an unpleasant impression on Tennyson. Yet that his objection would have extended to a study such as the present I cannot believe. Indeed, he himself leans to the contrary position when he says, a few lines above the passage first quoted:

'Far indeed am I from asserting that books as well as Nature are not, and ought not to be, suggestive to the poet. I am sure that I myself, and many others, find a peculiar charm in those passages of such great masters as Virgil or Milton where they adopt the creation of a bygone poet, and reclothe it, more or less, according to their own fancy.'

Now with just such instances as these the present study aims to deal. It was not undertaken with the purpose of picking out trivial chance resemblances between Horace and other poets, in order to substantiate a charge of plagiarism; the purpose is rather to find the 'reclothings' of which Tennyson speaks, and from them to infer the

[1] *Alfred Lord Tennyson* 2. 385.

influence of Horace upon a great epoch of English poetry. 'My para-phrases of certain Latin and Greek lines seem too obvious to be men-tioned,' says Tennyson in the brief prefatory notes to his collected works. No one would accuse him of plagiarism on account of such paraphrases; yet from them can be gleaned material of value about his tastes in literature. According to his own statement, a poet should be known by his works.

Such characteristics as Horace and Tennyson have in common have frequently been noticed by others. C. S. Calverley[1] calls atten-tion to one group:

'Between Horace, especially, and the modern poet there exist, we think, in point of style and workmanship, many similarities. A stanza of *In Memoriam* is a thing compact, *teres atque rotundus*, as is a stanza in a Horatian ode. Both writers are equally intolerant of any but the right word, and both have the gift of making it fit into its place apparently by a happy accident. The condensed phraseology, the abruptness, the ease (attained probably *per laborem plurimum*, until art became a second nature) which characterize the *Odes* of Horace characterize the cantos, so to call them, of *In Memoriam*. Even Mr. Tennyson's compound epithets are paralleled, and more than paralleled, in Horace.'

To turn from similarities of technique to similarities of tempera-ment, we find Andrew Lang[2] saying of Tennyson: 'He constantly reminds us of Virgil, Homer, Theocritus, and even Persius and Horace.'

And though the coupling of Horace with Persius would indicate that Lang had Horace the satirist in mind, the truth is that Tennyson even more often reminds us of Horace the lyrist. As Palgrave, says:[3]

'It was, indeed, more than most poets that Tennyson (as justly has been remarked about Horace) felt the two impulses described by M. Arnold, one driving the poet "to the world without" and "one to solitude"; although the happier circumstances of Tennyson's life allowed him less of Rome and more of Tibur and the Sabine farm than fell to the lot of the great Italian.'

But more convincing than any of these statements, I venture to

[1] *Works*, London, 1901, pp. 508-509.
[2] *Alfred Tennyson (Modern English Writers)*, p. 223.
[3] See Hallam Tennyson, *Alfred Lord Tennyson* 2. 489.

hope, will be an examination of the actual resemblances found between the poetry of Horace and that of Tennyson, since they are so many, and so much a part of the latter's work.

Browning. Browning, the son of cultivated and talented parents, had every opportunity to form an early acquaintance with Horace. His father, we are told, 'knew by heart . . . all the *Odes* of Horace,'[1] and he could hardly have failed to make his son familiar with a favorite author. When the poet was twelve years old, his uncle, Reuben Browning, presented him with Christopher Smart's translation of Horace[2]—a version which, though not always felicitous, has the advantage of being in prose, and is fairly accurate. Browning may have been thinking of this gift when, more than sixty years later, in his *Parleyings with Certain People of Importance* (*Parleyings with Christopher Smart*), he mentioned as an 'unsightly bough':

> Smart's who translated Horace.

But it is unlikely that the poet did not know something of Horace long before he was twelve—and that, too, in no translation, but in the original Latin. His biographer, William Sharp, says (though I have not been able to find other authority for the statement) that Browning at the age of eight 'began to translate the simpler odes of Horace.'[3] These early translations, as well as the Horatian ode which Sharp in the same paragraph tells us the ten-year-old Browning wrote in honor of his first sweetheart, have disappeared, with the rest of the poet's juvenile efforts. The only translation of any considerable portion of Horace found in Browning's extant works (the version of part of *Carm.* 1. 3 in *Fifine at the Fair*) is literal and accurate.

For better evidence of Browning's knowledge of Horace we turn to his own poetry, where on occasion he quotes the Roman with a fluency and readiness equalled by few. We are almost inclined to attribute to him his father's extraordinary acquaintance with our poet, so easily do the phrases come to him—and phrases not always the most familiar. Yet mark that it is 'on occasion.' In large proportion, the numerous citations from Horace in Browning's poems are found in the ninth and tenth books of *The Ring and the Book*[4]—comprising the

---

[1] Mrs. Sutherland Orr, *Robert Browning* 1. 16.

[2] Griffin and Minchin, *Life of Robert Browning*, p. 6.

[3] *Life of Robert Browning*, p. 26.

[4] Lest it should be thought that the quotations from Horace occur in Browning's original, I may note here that I have examined *The Old Yellow Book*, and find no trace of Horace in the lawyers' papers.

briefs of the two advocates. The poet, able to quote to an unlimited extent when he so desires, is equally able to suppress any trace of Horace for hundreds of pages.

There is an explanation for this. Browning is one of those authors who are little given to self-revelation; he disapproves of a poet's 'unlocking his heart' to a curious world — 'if so, the less Shakespeare he!' As for himself, he seldom speaks *in propria persona* in his poems. In fact, although Browning's finest work is not found in his plays, his genius is essentially dramatic so far as regards treatment of character. The poet has the faculty of altogether identifying himself, Robert Browning, with Fra Lippo Lippi, or with the duke who exhibits his dead wife's picture, or with the dying bishop. We do not even know the names of many of his personages; but we do know the persons, and the workings of their minds and souls, as we do not know their creator. Generalities, of course, we can determine; as the fact that Browning was more interested in the inner nature of human beings than in anything else in the universe. But what were his own thoughts and feelings about many subjects on which he writes must remain a blank to us. So it is that when he is impersonating Dominus Hyacinthus de Archangelis, or Juris Doctor Johannes-Baptista Bottinius, he quotes a great deal of Horace because it seems appropriate that these advocates steeped in Latin should be for ever showing their classical erudition; whereas, when he turns to other characters, he endows them with other knowledge, or with none at all, to suit his purpose.

We must allow, then, that the large amount of Horace found in Browning is for the most part not a characteristic element in his work. Indeed, Browning was really little influenced by any one. Sources he often had and used, of course; but of genuine influence upon his poetry, such as that of Milton upon Wordsworth, or of Spenser upon Keats, there is almost none. Browning—though it may sound rather paradoxical after all that has been said — is emphatically himself; rarely can a line of his poetry be mistaken for the work of any one else. In his letters, where, if anywhere, we look for the real Robert Browning, he seldom quotes; it is as if he had so much of his own to say that what others have said does not occur to him. The same reason explains the rapidity with which he wrote — a rapidity which sometimes lends support to the charge of obscurity, and which certainly is foreign to Horace. Unlike Horace, too, are the self-concealment which we have noticed, and the buoyant optimism which recurs so constantly that we can safely point to it as one of Browning's characteristics. Though at first thought we might say the two poets were alike in their deep interest in human nature, we soon see that even here their attitudes are different: Horace is interested in what he sees the men about him doing; Browning cares for their deeds only in so far as they reveal their thoughts and help him to understand their souls. With him, in very truth, ' 'tis not what man does that exalts him, but what man would do.'

With Browning we reach the last of the great English poets of the nineteenth century. Many lesser singers there were, but none who could rank with the seven here discussed. Nor are these all of equal merit; yet each plays a considerable part in the literature of his country, and for the present, at least, demands our attention. No one can predict what the judgment of succeeding ages may be. Horace's place in the world's culture is secure; but these others 'abide our question.' Not all of them, as we have seen, cared for Horace or understood him; but all knew him, and almost all used him. His many-sidedness, which after all is his chief claim to distinction, makes it virtually impossible for any one person to appreciate him fully. Yet it also gives nearly every one something in common with him, and ensures the permanence of his fame, which has indeed been *aere perennius*.

The following pages record the resemblances I have found between

Details concerning this Study.
Horace and the seven poets. In making this record I have, except in cases where there are other obvious traces, disregarded such commonplaces as 'the golden mean,' 'the man of fixed and virtuous will,' the immortality conferred by poetry, and so on, since these have been so often used as to be no longer the property of Horace, but of the world. I have also refrained from citing chance Horace-like phrases in the prose of Byron and Coleridge; these two were so prone to scatter fragments of Latin — often only a word or two — throughout their writings that we cannot justly ascribe every such occurrence to the influence of a particular Latin author. The habit merely shows a facile memory providing a familiar catchword. All the important citations in their prose I have noted; and, of course, every one, no matter how slight, in their poetry. Finally, I have normalized the spelling and punctuation of all quotations throughout the thesis, except where the poets themselves quote Horace inexactly; in all such cases I have noted the deviation from the accepted text.

WILLIAM WORDSWORTH

I. *Unquestionable traces of Horace*

(1) Motto of *Ode* (1814):

> Carmina possumus
> Donare, et pretium dicere muneri.
> Non incisa notis marmora publicis,
> Per quae spiritus et vita redit bonis
> Post mortem ducibus . . . . .
> . . . . clarius indicant
> Laudes quam . . . Pierides; neque
> Si chartae sileant quod bene feceris
> Mercedem tuleris.
>
> (*Carm.* 4. 8. 11 ff.)

(For *muneri* read *muneris*.)

(2) Compare with this passage from Horace the following lines (100 ff.) from Wordsworth's *Ode* (1814):

> And be the guardian spaces
> Of consecrated places
> As nobly graced by Sculpture's patient toil;
> And let imperishable Columns rise
> Fixed in the depths of this courageous soil;
> Expressive signals of a glorious strife,
> And competent to shed a spark divine
> Into the torpid breast of daily life.
>
> . . . .
> And ye, Pierian Sisters, ...
>
> . . . .
> Chanting for patriot heroes the reward
> Of never-dying song!
>
> . . . .
> So shall the characters of that proud page
> Support their mighty theme from age to age;
> And, in the desert places of the earth,
> When they to future empires have given birth,
> So shall the people gather and believe
> The bold report, transferred to every clime.

(3) Motto of the sonnet beginning, 'The feudal Keep, the bastions of Cohorn':

> Dignum laude virum Musa vetat mori.

See *Carm.* 4. 8. 28.

(4)   Footnote to *Plea for the Historian,* which ends with the lines:

> And taught her [Clio's] faithful servants how the lyre
> Should animate, but not mislead, the pen:
>
> Quem virum . . . . lyra . . . .
> . . . . . sumes [*sic*] celebrare, Clio?

See *Carm.* 1. 12. 1-2.   (For *sumes* read *sumis.*)

(5)   From the sonnet beginning, 'Young England—what is then become of Old,' ll. 10-11:

> An imitative race,
> The *servum pecus* of a Gallic breed.

See *Epist.* 1. 19. 19: *o imitatores, servum pecus.*

(6)   Footnote to a sentence in the *Guide through the Lake District* (the sentence reads: 'Sufficient specimens remain to give a high gratification to the man of genuine taste.'):

> 'Written some time ago. The injury done since is more than
> could have been calculated upon. *Singula de nobis anni praedantur
> euntes.*'

See *Epist.* 2. 2. 55.

(7)   Motto of the prose tractate entitled *Concerning the Relations of Great Britain, Spain, and Portugal to Each Other and to the Common Enemy at this Crisis; and Specifically as Affected by the Convention of Cintra*:

> Qui didicit patriae quid debeat, . . .
> Quod sit conscripti, quod iudicis officium, quae
> Partes in bellum missi ducis.

See *Ars Poet.* 312 ff.

(8)   From the preface to the edition of the poems published in 1815:

> ' "So seemed," and to whom seemed? To the heavenly Muse
> who dictates the poem, to the eye of the Poet's mind, and to that of the
> reader, present at one moment in the wide Ethiopian, and the next in
> the solitudes, then first broken in upon, of the infernal regions!
> Modo me Thebis, modo ponit Athenis.'

See *Epist.* 2. 1. 213.

(9)   From a letter to William Mathews, June, 1791:

> 'I quitted London about three weeks ago, where my time passed in
> a strange manner; sometimes whirled about by the vortex of its *strenua
> inertia.*'

See *Epist.* 1. 11. 28: *strenua nos exercet inertia.*

(10)   From a letter to the same, March, 1796:

'These [Juvenal, Horace, Boileau, Pope, "the redoubted Peter"]
are great names, but to myself I shall apply the passage of Horace,
changing the bee into a wasp to suit the subject.
                        Ego apis Matinae
                        More modoque,
                                             etc., etc.'

See *Carm*. 4. 2. 27-28.

(11)   From a letter to John Scott, March, 1816 (referring to
Brougham):

'Our last interview was terminated among the majestic woods of
Lowther, near his own beautiful residence. Thither I would gladly
remit him *inter silvas Academi quaerere verum*.'

See *Epist*. 2. 2. 45.

(12)   From a letter to the same, April, 1816:

'What a difference between the *amabilis insania* of inspiration,
and the fiend-like exasperation of these wretched productions.'

See *Carm*. 3. 4. 5-6.

(13)   From a letter to R. P. Gillies, April, 1816:

'Do not let anybody persuade you that any quantity of good verses
can be produced by mere felicity; or that an immortal style can be the
growth of mere genius. *Multa tulit fecitque* must be the motto of all
those who are to last.'

See *Ars Poet*. 413.

(14)   From a letter to Lord Lonsdale, February, 1819 (discussing
Wordsworth's translation of a passage from the *Aeneid*):

'These two lines will be deemed, I apprehend, hard and bald.   So
true is Horace's remark, *in vitium ducet* [*sic*] *culpae fuga*, etc.'

See *Ars Poet*. 31.   (For *ducet* read *ducit*.)

(15)   From a letter to Barron Field, October, 1828:

'The word "rebounds" I wish much to introduce here [in the poem
beginning, "Yes, it was the mountain Echo"]; for the imaginative
warning turns upon the echo, which ought to be revived as near the
conclusion as possible. This rule of art holds equally good as to the
theme of a piece of music, as in a poem.
                Prima dicte mihi summa dicende Camaena [*sic*].
                                             (*Epist*. 1. 1. 1.)'

(For *Camaena* read *Camena*.)

(16)   From a letter to John Peace, January, 1841 (speaking of 'the
inextinguishable love of the country as manifested by the inhabitants

of cities in their culture of plants and flowers'):

> 'The germ of the main thought is to be found in Horace:
> Nempe inter varias nutritur silva columnas,
> Laudaturque domus longos quae prospicit agros.
> Naturam expellas furca, tamen usque recurret.
> (*Epist.* 1. 10. 22-24.)'

(17)   From a letter to Henry Reed, August, 1841:

> 'Our two present Philosophes [Emerson and Carlyle], who have
> taken a language which they suppose to be English for their vehicle,
> are verily *par nobile fratrum*, and it is a pity that the weakness of our
> age has not left them exclusively to this appropriate reward—mutual
> admiration.'

See *Serm.* 2. 3. 243.

(18)   From a letter to Sir Robert Peel, April, 1843:

> 'Having since my first acquaintance with Horace borne in mind
> the charge which he tells us frequently thrilled his ear:
> Solve senescentem mature sanus equum, ne
> Peccet ad extremum.'

See *Epist.* 1. 1. 8-9.

(19)   From *An Evening Walk*, ll. 72-77:

> Did Sabine grace adorn my living line,
> Bandusia's praise, wild stream, should yield to thine!
> Never shall ruthless minister of death
> 'Mid thy soft glooms the glittering steel unsheath;
> No goblets shall, for thee, be crowned with flowers,
> No kid with piteous outcry thrill thy bowers.

See *Carm.* 3. 13:

> O fons Bandusiae, splendidior vitro,
> Dulci digne mero non sine floribus,
>   Cras donaberis haedo,
>   Cui frons turgida cornibus
> Primis et venerem et proelia destinat;
> Frustra: nam gelidos inficiet tibi
>   Rubro sanguine rivos
>   Lascivi suboles gregis.
> Te flagrantis atrox hora Caniculae
> Nescit tangere, tu frigus amabile
>   Fessis vomere tauris
>   Praebes et pecori vago.
> Fies nobilium tu quoque fontium,
> Me dicente cavis impositam ilicem
>   Saxis, unde loquaces
>   Lymphae desiliunt tuae.

(20) From *The River Duddon* 1. 1-4:

> Not envying Latian shades—if yet they throw
> A grateful coolness round that crystal Spring,
> Bandusia, prattling as when long ago
> The Sabine Bard was moved her praise to sing.

See the ode (3. 13) quoted above.

(21) From *Musings near Aquapendente*, ll. 255-262:

> Or Sabine vales explored inspire a wish
> To meet the shade of Horace by the side
> Of his Bandusian fount; or I invoke
> His presence to point out the spot where once
> He sate, and eulogized with earnest pen
> Peace, leisure, freedom, moderate desires;
> And all the immunities of rural life
> Extolled, behind Vacuna's crumbling fane.

The first part of this refers, of course, to *Carm.* 3. 13; the latter part, beginning with line 258, is inspired by *Epist.* 1. 10. The epistle need not be quoted entire; several lines will suffice to show where Wordsworth finds his material:

> Ego laudo ruris amoeni
> Rivos et musco circumlita saxa nemusque.
> Quid quaeris? Vivo et regno, simul ista reliqui,
> Quae vos ad caelum fertis rumore secundo:
>
> . . . .
> . . . Fuge magna; licet sub paupere tecto
> Reges et regum vita praecurrere amicos.
>
> . . . .
> Sic, qui pauperiem veritus potiore metallis
> Libertate caret, dominum vehit improbus atque
> Serviet aeternum, quia parvo nesciet uti.
>
> . . . .
> Haec tibi dictabam post fanum putre Vacunae.
>
> (*Epist.* 1. 10. 6 ff.)

(22) From *Liberty*, ll. 89-110:

> A pure life uncrossed
> By cares in which simplicity is lost.
> That life—the flowery path that winds by stealth—
> Which Horace needed for his spirit's health;
> Sighed for, in heart and genius overcome
> By noise and strife and questions wearisome,
> And the vain splendors of Imperial Rome.—
> Let easy mirth his social hours inspire,
> And fiction animate his sportive lyre,

> Attuned to verse that, crowning light Distress
> With garlands, cheats her into happiness;
> Give *me* the humblest note of those sad strains
> Drawn forth by pressure of his gilded chains,
> As a chance-sunbeam from his memory fell
> Upon the Sabine farm he loved so well;
> Or when the prattle of Bandusia's spring
> Haunted his ear—he only listening—
> He proud to please, above all rivals, fit
> To win the palm of gaiety and wit;
> He, doubt not, with involuntary dread,
> Shrinking from each new favor to be shed,
> By the world's Ruler, on his honored head.

There are many reminiscences of Horace in this passage. 'Bandusia's spring,' line 104, will at once be recognized (*Carm*. 3. 13). The 'Sabine farm,' line 103, is celebrated by its owner in *Carm*. 2. 16. 37; 2. 18. 14; 3. 1. 47; *Serm*. 2. 7. 118; *Epist*. 1. 14; 1. 16. 'Noise and strife' (l. 94) is an echo of *Carm*. 3. 29. 12: *fumum et opes strepitumque Romae*. For 'questions wearisome' (l. 94) see *Serm*. 2. 6. 29 ff. 'The flowery path that winds by stealth' (l. 91) paraphrases *Epist*. 1. 18. 103: *secretum iter et fallentis semita vitae*. The 'sportive lyre' of line 97 is from *Carm*. 3. 3. 69: *iocosae lyrae*. It is hardly necessary to add that besides these specific references, the theme of the Wordsworthian passage is frequent in Horace.

(23)   From *The Prelude* 8. 173 ff.:

> Smooth life had flock and shepherd in old time,
> Long springs and tepid winters on the banks
> Of delicate Galesus. .   .   .   .
> .   .   .   .   .   . And the goat-herd lived
> As calmly, underneath the pleasant brows
> Of cool Lucretilis, where the pipe was heard
> Of Pan, Invisible God, thrilling the rocks
> With tutelary music, from all harm
> The fold protecting.

See *Carm*. 2. 6. 10 ff.:

> Dulce pellitis ovibus Galaesi
> Flumen .   .   .   petam, .   .   .
> Ver ubi longum tepidasque praebet
> Iuppiter brumas;

and *Carm*. 1. 17. 1 ff.:

> Velox amoenum saepe Lucretilem
> Mutat Lycaeo Faunus et igneam

Defendit aestatem capellis
Usque meis pluviosque ventos.
Impune tutum per nemus arbutos
Quaerunt, ...
Utcumque dulci, Tyndari, fistula
. . . .
Levia personuere saxa.

(24) From the poem beginning, 'Departing summer hath assumed,' ll. 37 ff.:

Nor such the spirit-stirring note
When the live chords Alcaeus smote,
Inflamed by sense of wrong;
Woe! woe to Tyrants! from the lyre
Broke threateningly, in sparkles dire
Of fierce vindictive song.

And not unhallowed was the page
By wingèd Love inscribed, to assuage
The pangs of vain pursuit;
Love listening while the Lesbian Maid
With finest touch of passion swayed
Her own Aeolian lute.

O ye, who patiently explore
The wreck of Herculanean lore,
What rapture! could ye seize
Some Theban fragment, or unroll
One precious, tender-hearted scroll
Of pure Simonides.

That were, indeed, a genuine birth
Of poesy: . . . .
What Horace gloried to behold,
. . . . shall we enfold?
Can haughty Time be just?

These lines may be traced to the following passages in Horace

Non . . . .
⁎ . . . . . Pindaricae latent
Ceaeque¹ et Alcaei minaces
Stesichorique graves Camenae.

(*Carm.* 4. 9. 5-8.)

Spirat adhuc amor
Vivuntque commissi calores
Aeoliae fidibus puellae.

(*Carm.* 4. 9. 10-12.)

¹ Simonides of Ceos.

Aeoliis fidibus querentem
Sappho puellis de popularibus,
Et te sonantem plenius aureo,
Alcaee, plectro dura navis,
Dura fugae mala, dura belli!

(*Carm.* 2. 13. 24 ff.)

Wordsworth has expanded the ideas which he took from these verses, but his points of departure are clear. The germ of 'the spirit-stirring note' and 'the live chords' lies in *sonantem plenius*; lines 40-42 are based on *Alcaei minaces*; lines 43-48 go back to the second quotation from Horace, although the source of 'Aeolian lute' is probably the *Aeoliis fidibus* of the third quotation.

(25)   From the early poem beginning, 'And has the Sun his flaming chariot driven,' l. 13:

Emerging slow from Academus' grove.

See *Epist.* 2. 2. 45:

Atque inter silvas Academi.

(26)   Wordsworth again echoes this line in *Dion*, l. 10:

Fell round him in the grove of Academe.

(27)   From *Stanzas Composed in the Simplon Pass*, l. 3:

Anio's precipitous flood.

See *Carm.* 1. 7. 13: *praeceps Anio.*

(28)   From *The Prelude* 2. 78:

Our daily meals were frugal, Sabine fare!

This refers to Horace's descriptions of the simplicity with which he lived on his Sabine farm (see above, p. 54); there may also be a specific reminiscence of *Carm.* 1. 20. 1:

Vile potabis . . . . Sabinum.

(29)   From the poem beginning, 'This Lawn, a carpet all alive,' ll. 5-6:

Worldlings revelling in the fields
Of strenuous idleness.

See *Epist.* 1. 11. 28: *strenua inertia.*

(30)   From *The Prelude* 4. 377-378:

Making night do penance for a day
Spent in a round of strenuous idleness.

See the preceding reference to Horace.

(31)   Of his *Ode to Duty* Wordsworth says:

'This Ode is on the model of Gray's Ode to Adversity, which is copied from Horace's Ode to Fortune.'

The hymn to Fortune (*Carm.* 1. 35) begins by describing the omnipotence of the goddess. There follows the mention of those who are under her sway, including, of course, all classes of men. Next come descriptions of her forerunner, Necessity, and her friends, Hope and Honor. The poet then speaks of the fickleness of the *volgus infidum*, which shuns those who have suffered reverses, and thus is false to Fortune. He prays the goddess to protect Caesar, and ends with a lament for the civil wars, and a wish that Roman swords might be turned against a foreign enemy.

Gray, in his *Hymn to Adversity*, follows the plan of Horace, and is sometimes reminiscent of his language, as in 'purple Tyrants' (*purpurei tyranni*). Adversity, like Fortune, has power over every one. 'Folly's idle brood' fly at her frown; but Wisdom, Melancholy, Charity, Justice, and Pity attend her. She is besought to be gentle to her suppliant; and the poet ends by saying:

> The generous spark extinct revive,
> Teach me to love and to forgive,
> Exact my own defects to scan,
> What others feel, and know myself a Man.

The details which Wordsworth's *Ode to Duty* has in common with these two poems are the idea of the omnipotence of the being who is the subject of the ode, and the prayer for the gracious favor of this being. To quote:

> Who art a light to guide, a rod
> To check the erring, and reprove;
> Thou, who art victory and law
> When empty terrors overawe;

and:

> Oh! if through confidence misplaced
> They fail, thy saving arms, dread Power! around them cast.
>
> Give unto me, made lowly wise,
> The spirit of self-sacrifice;
> The confidence of reason give;
> And in the light of truth thy Bondman let me live!

Also the lines,

> Flowers laugh before thee on their beds
> And fragrance in thy footing treads,

probably go back to the theme of the attendants of Fortune and Adversity represented in the other two odes. And the first line of the poem,

> Stern Daughter of the Voice of God!

is an invocation, as is the Horatian

> O diva, gratum quae regis Antium!

II. *Probable traces of Horace*

(1)   From *The Two April Mornings*, ll. 49-50:

> No fountain from its rocky cave
> E'er tripped with foot so free.

See *Carm.* 3. 13. 14-16:

> Me dicente cavis impositam ilicem
> Saxis, unde loquaces
> Lymphae desiliunt tuae;

and *Epod.* 16. 47-48:

> Montibus altis
> Levis crepante lympha desilit pede.

(2)   From the sonnet *Occasioned by the Battle of Waterloo*, ll. 6-7:

> Death, becoming death, is dearer far,
> When duty bids you bleed in open war.

See *Carm.* 3. 2. 13:

> Dulce et decorum est pro patria mori.

(Note especially 'becoming' and *decorum*.)

(3)   From *Dion*, l. 71:

> Like Auster whirling to and fro.

This probably may be traced to the Horatian *turbidus Auster* of *Carm.* 3. 3. 4-5; for it will be remembered that *turbidus* has the same root as *turbo*, a whirlwind.

(4)   From *Processions*, ll. 33-35:

> And a deeper dread
> Scattered on all sides by the hideous jars
> Of Corybantian cymbals.

See *Carm.* 1. 16. 7-8:

> Non acuta
> Sic geminant Corybantes aera.

(5)   From the poem beginning, 'Departing summer hath assumed,' ll. 15 ff.:

> Fall, rosy garlands, from my head!
> Ye myrtle wreaths, your fragrance shed
> Around a younger brow!

These lines are perhaps based on *Carm.* 1. 38:

> Persicos odi, puer, apparatus
> Displicent nexae philyra coronae;
> Mitte sectari, rosa quo locorum
> Sera moretur;
> Simplici myrto nihil adlabores
> Sedulus curo: neque te ministrum
> Dedecet myrtus neque me sub arta
> Vite bibentem.

The application is not the same; but the juxtaposition of the 'rosy garlands' and the 'myrtle wreaths' makes it very probable that Wordsworth, having, as we know,[1] Horace in mind while composing his poem, recalled at the moment this familiar little ode. Horace, a poet, speaks of roses and myrtle as likely to be used by him; Wordsworth, declaring that his days of high poetic inspiration are past, uses these as symbolic of a power that is deserting him.

(6) From *Inscriptions Supposed to be Found in and near a Hermit's Cell* 4. 9-10:

> Parching summer hath no warrant
> To consume this crystal Well.

See *Carm.* 3. 13. 9-10:

> Te [fontem Bandusiae] flagrantis atrox hora Caniculae
> Nescit tangere.

(7) From *Personal Talk*, ll. 55-56:

> Oh! might my name be numbered among theirs [the Poets'],
> Then gladly would I end my mortal days.

See *Carm.* 1. 1. 35-36:

> Quod si me lyricis vatibus inseres,
> Sublimi feriam sidera vertice.

(8) From *Extempore Effusion upon the Death of James Hogg*, ll. 21-24:

> Like clouds that rake the mountain-summits,
> Or waves that own no curbing hand,
> How fast has brother followed brother,
> From sunshine to the sunless land!

See *Epist.* 2. 2. 175-176:

> Sic quia perpetuus nulli datur usus, et heres
> Heredem alterius velut unda supervenit undam.

---

[1] See above, pp. 55-56.

There are two points of similarity between the two passages—the simile of the waves, and the phrases, 'brother followed brother' and *heres heredem supervenit*.   Either of these taken separately might imply nothing; but found in such close conjunction in both cases, they suggest the possibility of a reminiscence.

(9)   From *Written in March*, ll. 11-12:

> Like an army defeated
> The snow hath retreated.

See *Carm.* 4. 7. 1:

> Diffugere nives.

(10)   From the sonnet beginning, 'From the dark chambers of dejection freed,' ll. 7-10:

> Yet a rich guerdon waits on minds that dare,
> If aught be in them of immortal seed,
> And reason govern that audacious flight
> Which heavenward they direct.

See *Carm.* 3. 4. 65 ff.:

> Vis consili expers mole ruit sua:
> Vim temperatum di quoque provehunt
> In maius.

The 'minds that dare,' governed by 'reason,' is perhaps an echo of the Horatian *vim temperatum*, with a backward look at the *consili* of the preceding line.

(11)   From a letter to Francis Wrangham (February, 1819):

> 'Dear Wrangham, are you and I ever likely to meet in this world again?   Yours is a *corner* of the earth; mine is not so.'

The italics of the word 'corner,' which seem to have some particular significance, suggest a comparison with *Carm.* 2. 6. 13-14:

> Ille terrarum mihi praeter omnes
> Angulus ridet.

SAMUEL TAYLOR COLERIDGE

I. Unquestionable traces of Horace

(1) From *Table Talk*, May 14, 1833:

'If Wilson cares for fame, for an enduring place and prominence in literature, he should now, I think, hold his hand, and say, as he well may:

> *Militavi* non sine gloria;
> Nunc arma defunctumque *bello*
> Barbiton hic paries habebit.'

See *Carm*. 3. 26. 2-4.

(2) From a review in *The Morning Post*, March 27, 1800:

'He [Arthur Young] hastened to avow his recantation in a work almost lyrically unconnected, and set to a more boisterous music than would have suited any species of the Lyric, except the *Palinodia*.

> Quid amplius vis? O mare! O terra! ardeo,
> Quantum neque atro delibutus Hercules
> Nessi cruore . . . .
> Quae finis aut quod me manet *stipendium?*
> (*Epod*. 17.)'

See *Epod*. 17. 30-36 (abridged, and a slight alteration in l. 30, where we should read *et terra* for *O terra*).

(3) From a contribution to *The Courier*, June 4, 1811:

'The inhabitants of the Peninsula are our *friends*, and we cannot permit our own boys to tell us from their school-books:

> Absentem qui laedit, amicum
> Qui non *defendit* alio culpante,—
> *Hic niger est!*'

See *Serm*. 1. 4. 81-85. (Abridged. For *laedit* read *rodit*.)

(4) From a note to a sentence in *A Lay Sermon* (the sentence reads: 'It is well known, and has been observed of old, that poetry tends to render its devotees careless of money and outward appearances.'):

> Hic error tamen et levis haec insania quantas
> Virtutes habeat, sic collige. Vatis avarus
> Non temere est animus; versus amat, hoc studet unum;
> Detrimenta, fugas servorum, incendia ridet;
> Non fraudem socio puerove incogitat ullam
> Pupillo; vivit siliquis et pane secundo;
> Militiae quamquam piger et malus, utilis urbi.
> (*Epist*. 2. 1. 118[ff.])

(5)   From a suppressed passage in *The Friend:*

> 'Conscious that I am about to deliver my sentiments on a subject
> of the utmost delicacy—to walk
>
>   per ignes
>   Suppositos cineri doloso—
> I have been tempted by my fears to preface them with a motto of
> unusual length.'

See *Carm.* 2. 1. 7-8.

(6)   From *A Lay Sermon:*

> 'This accomplished man of the world has given an account of the
> subjects of conversation between the illustrious statesmen who
> governed, and the brightest luminaries who then adorned, the empire
> of the civilized world:
>
>   Sermo oritur, non de villis domibusve alienis,
>   Nec male necne Lepos saltet; sed quod magis ad nos
>   Pertinet et nescire malum est, agitamus: utrumne
>   Divitiis homines an sint virtute beati,
>   . . . .
>   Et quod sit natura boni summumque quid eius.
>   (*Serm.* 2. 6. 71 ff.)'

(For *quod* in the last line read *quae*.)

(7)   Motto of poem, *To the Rev. George Coleridge:*

>   Notus in fratres animi paterni.
>   (*Carm.* 2. 2. [6.])

(8)   From *Anima Poetae,* 1806-1807:

> 'Serpentium adlapsus timet. Quaere—*allapse* of serpents. *Horace.*
> —What other word have we?'

See *Epod.* 1. 20.

(9)   Motto of *Reflections on Having Left a Place of Retirement:*

>   'Sermoni propriora.—Hor.'

See *Serm.* 1. 4. 42.   (For *propriora* read *propiora*.)

(10)   The same phrase is used in a note appended to an autograph
manuscript of *Fears in Solitude.*

(11)   From an essay *On the Third Possible Church:*

> '*Mons adhuc parturit:* the *ridiculus mus* was but an omen.'

See *Ars Poet.* 139: *parturient montes, nascetur ridiculus mus.*

(12)   From *Biographia Literaria,* chapter 2:

> 'They [readers] in general apply to *all* poets the old sarcasm of
> Horace upon the scribblers of his time: *Genus irritabile vatum.*'

See *Epist.* 2. 2. 102.

(13) From *Vindication of Southey:*

—'Any man that daily reverences the old Horatian verdict:
Who basely wounds an *absent* friend's fair fame,
Or skulks from his defense when others blame,
Is—

but we leave the completing line to be translated in private by those
whom it may concern.'

See *Serm.* 1. 4. 81 ff.—quoted above, No. 3.

(14) The title of the poem *Dura Navis* is from *Carm.* 2. 13. 27.

(15) From a note to the same poem:

'Old Jemmy Boyer, the plagose Orbilius of Christ's Hospital.'

See *Epist.* 2. 1. 70-71: *plagosum Orbilium.*

(16) From *Talleyrand to Lord Grenville*, ll. 35-36:

No time from my name this my motto shall sever:
'Twill be *Non sine pulvere palma* for ever.

See *Epist.* 1. 1. 51:

Cui sit condicio dulcis sine pulvere palmae?

(17) From *Nonsense Sapphics*:

Here's Jem's first copy of nonsense verses,
All in the antique style of Mistress Sappho,
Latin just like Horace the tuneful Roman,
Sapph's imitator:

But we Bards, we classical Lyric Poets,
Know a thing or two in a scurvy Planet:
Don't we, now? Eh? Brother Horatius Flaccus,
Tip us your paw, Lad:

Here's to Maecenas and the other worthies;
Rich men of England! would ye be immortal?
Patronize Genius, giving Cash and Praise to
Gillman Jacobus.

II. Probable traces of Horace

(1) Title of a poem in Christ's Hospital book:

Nil Pejus Est Caelibe Vita.

See *Epist.* 1. 1. 88:

Melius nil caelibe vita.

(2)   From *Honour*, ll. 23-24:

> Or thunder at thy door the midnight train,
> Or Death shall knock that never knocks in vain.

See *Carm.* 1. 4. 13:

> Pallida mors aequo pulsat pede pauperum tabernas.

(3)   From *Easter Holidays*, l. 13:

> With mirthful dance they beat the ground.

See *Carm.* 1. 4. 7:

> Alterno terram quatiunt pede;

and *Carm.* 1. 37. 1-2:

> Nunc pede libero
> Pulsanda tellus.

(4)   First stanza of a poem called *Names*, adapted from Lessing:

> I ask'd my fair one happy day,
> What I should call her in my lay;
>   By what sweet name from Rome or Greece;
> Lalage, Neaera, Chloris,
> Sappho, Lesbia, or Doris,
>   Arethusa or Lucrece.

In the German the names are different.   Coleridge probably borrows Lalage and Neaera from Horace, who celebrates the former in *Carm.* 1. 22 and 2. 5, the latter in *Epod.* 15. 11.

LORD BYRON

I. Unquestionable traces of Horace

(1) Foremost in importance among the portions of Byron's writings that show a Horatian influence stands, of course, the *Hints from Horace*, which is, as the poet himself puts it, 'an allusion in English verse to the Epistle *Ad Pisones, De Arte Poetica*.' As we might expect, the first motto of the work is from the original:

> Ergo fungar vice cotis, acutum
> Reddere quae ferrum valet, exsors ipsa secandi.
> (*Ars Poet*. 304-305.)

It would not be to the purpose to transcribe here either the entire *Ars Poetica* or the whole of *Hints from Horace*. I shall therefore content myself with recording what seem to be the salient features of Byron's paraphrase. We have already remarked (see Introduction, p. 35) on the difference in tone between his version and the original; we may now take up more technical matters.

(a) Frequently Byron's renderings are so close as to deserve the name of translations; and sometimes they combine with this accuracy a surprising and delightful felicity. Take, for instance, ll. 99-100 of the Latin:

> Non satis est pulchra esse poemata; dulcia sunto
> Et, quocumque volent, animum auditoris agunto,

which reappears thus:

> 'Tis not enough, ye Bards, with all your art
> To polish poems;—they must touch the heart:
> Where'er the scene be laid, whate'er the song,
> Still let it bear the hearer's soul along.
> (Ll. 137-140.)

(b) Nearly always Byron substitutes English persons and places for the Greek and Latin examples of Horace; as ll. 52-57:

> Et nova fictaque nuper habebunt verba fidem, si
> Graeco fonte cadent parce detorta. Quid autem
> Caecilio Plautoque dabit Romanus ademptum
> Vergilio Varioque? Ego cur, adquirere pauca
> Si possum, invideor, cum lingua Catonis et Enni
> Sermonem patrium ditaverit,

which he renders:

> New words find credit in these latter days,
> If neatly grafted on a Gallic phrase;
> What Chaucer, Spenser did, we scarce refuse
> To Dryden's or to Pope's maturer Muse.
> If you can add a little, say why not,
> As well as William Pitt, and Walter Scott?
> Since they, by force of rhyme and force of lungs,
> Enriched our Island's ill-united tongues.

(Ll. 79-86.)

Possibly the happiest instance of this is the version of ll. 140-145:

> Quanto rectius hic qui nil molitur inepte:
> 'Dic mihi, Musa, virum, captae post tempora Troiae
> Qui mores hominum multorum vidit et urbes.'
> Non fumum ex fulgore, sed ex fumo dare lucem
> Cogitat, ut speciosa dehinc miracula promat,
> Antiphaten Scyllamque et cum Cyclope Charybdim;

which runs:

> Not so of yore awoke your mighty Sire
> The tempered warblings of his master-lyre;
> Soft as the gentler breathing of the lute,
> 'Of Man's first disobedience and the fruit'
> He speaks, but, as his subject swells along,
> Earth, Heaven, and Hades echo with the song.

(Ll. 199-204.)

Other substitutions are made for the sake of giving a modern flavor to the satire, as in the case of ll. 161-165:

> Imberbis iuvenis, tandem custode remoto,
> Gaudet equis canibusque et aprici gramine campi,
> Cereus in vitium flecti, monitoribus asper,
> Utilium tardus provisor, prodigus aeris,
> Sublimis cupidusque et amata relinquere pernix.

This Byron paraphrases:

> Behold him Freshman! forced no more to groan
> O'er Virgil's devilish verses and his own;
> Prayers are too tedious, Lectures too abstruse,
> He flies from Tavell's frown to 'Fordham's Mews';
> . . . .
> Fines, Tutors, tasks, Conventions threat in vain,
> Before hounds, hunters, and Newmarket Plain.
> Rough with his elders, with his equals rash,
> Civil to sharpers, prodigal of cash;
> Constant to nought—save hazard and a whore,

> Yet cursing both—for both have made him sore:
>
> . . . .
>
> Fooled, pillaged, dunned, he wastes his terms away,
> And unexpelled, perhaps, retires M. A.
>
> (Ll. 225-240.)

(c) In a few cases Byron would seem to have mistaken the meaning of a passage in the Latin; as in ll. 111-113:

> Post effert animi motus interprete lingua.
> Si dicentis erunt fortunis absona dicta,
> Romani tollent equites peditesque cachinnum,

which he renders:

> And for Expression's aid, 'tis said, or sung,
> She gave our mind's interpreter—the tongue,
> Who, worn with use, of late would fain dispense
> (At least in theaters) with common sense;
> O'erwhelm with sound the boxes, Gallery, Pit,
> And raise a laugh with anything—but Wit.

(d) Sometimes Byron's version of a passage is very free. Compare Horace (ll. 31-37) —

> In vitium ducit culpae fuga, si caret arte.
> Aemilium circa ludum faber imus et unguis
> Exprimet et mollis imitabitur aere capillos,
> Infelix operis summa, quia ponere totum
> Nesciet. Hunc ego me, siquid componere curem,
> Non magis esse velim, quam naso vivere pravo,
> Spectandum nigris oculis nigroque capillo—

with Byron:

> Unless your care's exact, your judgment nice,
> The flight from Folly leads but into Vice;
> None are complete, all wanting in some part,
> Like certain tailors, limited in art:
> For galligaskins Slowshears is your man,
> But coats must claim another artisan.
> Now this to me, I own, seems much the same
> As Vulcan's feet to bear Apollo's frame;
> Or, with a fair complexion, to expose
> Black eyes, black ringlets, but—a bottle nose.
>
> (Ll. 49-58.)

(e) At times we find Byron considerably abridging the Latin; for example, ll. 175-178,

> Multa ferunt anni venientes commoda secum,
> Multa recedentes adimunt. Ne forte seniles

> Mandentur iuveni partes pueroque viriles,
> Semper in adiunctis aevoque morabimur aptis,

have no counterpart in Byron's *Hints*.

(f)   Again, in some places Byron expands his original—much more, in fact, than in others he abridges it.   An instance of this is the passage, already quoted, describing the youthful collegian.   For another we may select ll. 193-201:

> Actoris partis chorus officiumque virile
> Defendat, neu quid medios intercinat actus
> Quod non proposito conducat et haereat apte.
> Ille bonis faveatque et consilietur amice
> Et regat iratos et amet pacare timentis;
> Ille dapes laudet mensae brevis, ille salubrem
> Iustitiam legesque et apertis otia portis;
> Ille tegat commissa deosque precetur et oret
> Ut redeat miseris, abeat fortuna superbis.

This is enlarged and altered to

> Of all the monstrous things I'd fain forbi d
> I loathe an Opera worse than Dennis did;
> Where good and evil persons, right or wrong,
> Rage, love, and aught but moralize—in song.
> Hail, last memorial of our foreign friends,
> Which Gaul allows, and still Hesperia lends!
> Napoleon's edicts no embargo lay
> On Whores—spies—singers—wisely shipped away.
> Our giant Capital, whose squares are spread
> Where rustics earned, and now may beg, their bread,
> In all iniquity is grown so nice,
> It scorns amusements which are not of price.
> Hence the pert shopkeeper, whose throbbing ear
> Aches with orchestras which he paid to hear,
> Whom shame, not sympathy, forbids to snore,
> His anguish doubling by his own 'encore';
> Squeezed in 'Fop's Alley,' jostled by the beaux,
> Teased with his hat, and trembling for his toes;
> Scarce wrestles through the night, nor tastes of ease,
> Till the dropped curtain gives a glad release:
> Why this, and more, he suffers—can ye guess?—
> Because it costs him dear, and makes him dress!

(Ll. 295-316.)

(g)   Finally, Byron frequently makes interpolations that have no basis whatever in Horace.   There is, for instance, the long diatribe on Jeffrey (ll. 589-626):

Again, my Jeffrey—as that sound inspires,
How wakes my bosom to its wonted fires!
Fires, such as gentle Caledonians feel
When Southrons writhe upon their critic wheel,
Or mild Eclectics, when some, worse than Turks,
Would rob poor Faith to decorate 'Good Works.'
Such are the genial feelings thou canst claim—
My Falcon flies not at ignoble game.
Mightiest of all Dunedin's beasts of chase!
For thee my Pegasus would mend his pace.
Arise, my Jeffrey! or my inkless pen
Shall never blunt its edge on meaner men;
Till thee or thine mine evil eye discerns,
'Alas! I cannot strike at wretched kernes.'
Inhuman Saxon! wilt thou then resign
A Muse and heart by choice so wholly thine?
Dear d—d contemner of my schoolboy songs,
Hast thou no vengeance for my Manhood's wrongs?
If unprovoked thou once could bid me bleed,
Hast thou no weapon for my daring deed?
What! not a word!—and am I then so low?
Wilt thou forbear, who never spared a foe?
Hast thou no wrath, or wish to give it vent?
No wit for Nobles, Dunces by descent?
No jest on 'minors,' quibbles on a name,
Nor one facetious paragraph of blame?
Is it for this on Ilion I have stood,
And thought of Homer less than Holyrood?
On shore of Euxine or Aegean sea,
My hate, untravelled, fondly turned to thee.
Ah! let me cease! in vain my bosom burns,
From Corydon unkind Alexis turns:
Thy rhymes are vain; thy Jeffrey then forego,
Nor woo that anger which he will not show.
What then?—Edina starves some lanker son,
To write an article thou canst not shun;
Some less fastidious Scotchman shall be found,
As bold in Billingsgate, though less renowned.

(2) So much for the *Hints*. Another Byronic adaptation of
Horace is from *Carm. 3. 3.* 1-8:

The man of firm and noble soul
No factious clamours can control;
No threat'ning tyrant's darkling brow
    Can swerve him from his just intent:
Gales the warring waves which plough,
    By Auster on the billows spent,

To curb the Adriatic main,
Would awe his fix'd, determin'd mind in vain.

Aye, and the red right arm of Jove,
Hurtling his lightnings from above,
With all his terrors there unfurl'd,
He would, unmov'd, unaw'd, behold.
The flames of an expiring world,
Again in crashing chaos roll'd,
In vast promiscuous ruin hurl'd,
Might light his glorious funeral pile:
Still dauntless 'midst the wreck of earth he'd smile.

The well-known original is as follows:

Iustum et tenacem propositi virum
Non civium ardor prava iubentium,
Non voltus instantis tyranni
Mente quatit solida, neque Auster,
Dux inquieti turbidus Hadriae,
Nec fulminantis magna manus Iovis;
Si fractus illabatur orbis,
Impavidum ferient ruinae.

(Note that Byron's 'red right arm' comes not from this ode, but from *Carm.* 1. 2. 2-3: *rubente dextera.*)

(3)   From *Childe Harold's Pilgrimage* 4. 74 and 77:

These hills seem things of lesser dignity;
All, save the lone Soracte's height, displayed
Not *now* in snow, which asks the lyric Roman's aid.
. . . .
Then farewell, Horace—whom I hated so,
Not for thy faults, but mine: it is a curse
To understand, not feel thy lyric flow,
To comprehend, but never love thy verse;
Although no deeper Moralist rehearse
Our little life, nor Bard prescribe his art,
Nor livelier Satirist the conscience pierce,
Awakening without wounding the touched heart,
Yet fare thee well—upon Soracte's ridge we part.

Horace's reference to Soracte is in *Carm.* 1. 9. 1-2:

Vides ut alta stet nive candidum
Soracte.

(4)   Motto of a poem addressed *To Edward Noel Long, Esq.:*

Nil ego contulerim iucundo sanus amico.

See *Serm.* 1. 5. 44.

(5). On the title-page of the 1807 edition of *Hours of Idleness* is printed:

> Virginibus puerisque canto.
>
> Horace.

See *Carm.* 3. 1. 4.

(6) Motto of *Marino Faliero:*

> *Dux* inquieti turbidus Hadriae.
>
> Horace.

See *Carm.* 3. 3. 5.

(7) From *The Blues* 1. 156:

> 'Tis high time for a *Sic me servavit Apollo*.

See *Serm.* 1. 9. 78.

(8) From *Don Juan* 1. 216:

> My days of love are over; me no more
>   The charms of maid, wife, and still less of widow,
> Can make the fool of which they made before,—
>   In short, I must not lead the life I did do;
> The credulous hope of mutual minds is o'er,
>   The copious use of claret is forbid too.

Byron appends this footnote:

> Me nec femina nec puer
>   Iam nec spes animi credula mutui,
> Nec certare iuvat mero
>   Nec vincire novis tempora floribus.
>
> (*Carm.* 4. 1. 30 [29-32].)

(9) From *Don Juan* 1. 212:

> *Non ego hoc ferrem calidus iuventa*
> *Consule Planco*, Horace said.

See *Carm.* 3. 14. 27-28.

(10) From *Don Juan* 14. 21:

> *Vetabo Cereris sacrum qui vulgarit—*
> Which means, that vulgar people must not share it.

See *Carm.* 3. 2. 26-27: *vetabo qui Cereris sacrum volgarit*.

(11) From *Don Juan* 13. 81:

> Or (to the point with Horace and with Pulci)
> *Omne tulit punctum*, quae *miscuit utile dulci*.

See *Ars Poet.* 343. (For *quae* read *qui*.)

(12) From *Don Juan* 1. 6:

> Most epic poets plunge *in medias res*
> (Horace makes this the heroic turnpike road).

See *Ars Poet.* 148.

(13) From *Don Juan* 13. 34-35:

> Perhaps we have borrowed this from the Chinese—
> Perhaps from Horace: his *Nil admirari*
> Was what he called the 'Art of Happiness.'

See *Epist.* 1. 6. 1-2.

(14) The same phrase is found in *Don Juan* 5. 100-101:

> And I must say, I ne'er could see the very
> Great happiness of the *Nil admirari*.

> 'Not to admire is all the art I know
> (Plain truth, dear Murray, needs few flowers of speech)
> To make men happy, or to keep them so';
> (So take it in the very words of Creech)—
> Thus Horace wrote we all know long ago;
> And thus Pope quotes the precept to reteach
> From his translation; but had *none admired*,
> Would Pope have sung, or Horace been inspired?

(15) From *Don Juan* 14. 77:

> *Beatus ille procul!* from *negotiis*,
> Saith Horace; the great little poet's wrong;
> His other maxim, *Noscitur a sociis*,
> Is much more to the purpose of his song;
> Though even that were sometimes too ferocious,
> Unless good company be kept too long.

See *Epod.* 2. 1:

> *Beatus ille qui procul negotiis.*

Byron makes a slip in attributing his other quotation to Horace; it is, so far as I can discover, of unknown origin.

(16) From *Don Juan* 6. 17:

> In short, the maxim for the amorous tribe is
> Horatian: *Medio tu tutissimus ibis.*

Again Byron is mistaken. The doctrine is Horatian, to be sure; but the words are from Ovid, *Metamorphoses* 2. 137.

(17) From *Don Juan* 9. 15:

> *O dura ilia messorum!*—'Oh
> Ye rigid guts of reapers!' I translate.

See *Epod.* 3. 4: *o dura messorum ilia.*

(18)   From *Don Juan* 9. 55:

> Oh thou *teterrima causa* of all *belli*—
> Thou gate of Life and Death—thou nondescript!

In a footnote Byron refers to *Serm.* 1. 3. 107-108.

(19)   From *Don Juan* 17. 10:

> Just as I make my mind up every day,
> To be a *totus*, *teres*, Stoic, Sage,
> The wind shifts and I fly into a rage.

See *Serm.* 2. 7. 86.

(20)   From *The Vision of Judgment*, l. 91:

> *Non di, non homines*—you know the rest.

See *Ars Poet.* 372-373:

> Mediocribus esse poetis
> Non homines, non di, non concessere columnae.

(21)   From the preface to *The Vision of Judgment:*

> 'However, it is worthy of him—*qualis ab incepto.*'

See *Ars Poet.* 127.

(22)   *My Boy Hobbie O* is signed

> ' *Infidus Scurra.*'

See *Epist.* 1. 18. 4: *infido scurrae distabit amicus.*

(23)   From *Don Juan* 12. 70:

> For Europe ploughs in Afric like *bos piger.*

See *Epist.* 1. 14. 43.

(24)   From *Don Juan* 11. 86:

> But *carpe diem*, Juan, *carpe, carpe!*

See *Carm.* 1. 11. 8.

(25)   From *Don Juan* 5. 63:

> Yet let them think that Horace has expressed
>   Shortly and sweetly the masonic folly
> Of those, forgetting the great place of rest,
>   Who give themselves to Architecture wholly;
> We know where things and men must end at best:
>   A moral (like all morals) melancholy,
> And *Et sepulchri immemor struis domos*
> Shows that we build when we should but entomb us.

See *Carm.* 2. 18. 18-19.

(26)   From *Don Juan* 11. 60:

> 'Tis strange the mind, that very fiery particle,
> Should let itself be snuffed out by an article.

Byron's own note on this is: '*Divinae particulam aurae*' — which comes from *Serm.* 2. 2. 79.

(27)   From *The Age of Bronze*, stanza 13:

> That nose, the hook where he suspends the world.

Byron's note is: '*Naso suspendis adunco.*—Horace.' See *Serm.* 1. 6. 5.

(28)   From *Werner* 2. 1. 19:

> Poor as a miser.

In writing to Murray, May 29, 1822, Byron says:

> 'Your printer has made one odd mistake—"poor as a *Mouse*" instead of "poor as a *Miser.*" The expression may seem strange, but it is only a translation of *Semper avarus eget.*'

See *Epist.* 1. 2. 56.

(29)   From a suppressed stanza of *Childe Harold's Pilgrimage* 1:

> While roared the blatant Beast, and roared, and raged, and—slept!!

Byron has the following note on this:

> ' "Blatant beast." A figure for the mob. I think first used by Smollett, in his *Adventures of an Atom.* Horace has the *bellua multorum capitum.*'

Though we may deplore the poet's ignorance of Spenser, we must accept his Horatian reference. We find in *Epist.* 1. 1. 76, *belua multorum es capitum.*

(30)   From *Childe Harold's Pilgrimage* 1 (*To Inez*):

> What Exile from himself can flee?

See *Carm.* 2. 16. 19-20:

> Patriae quis exsul
> Se quoque fugit?

(31)   From *Don Juan* 1. 5:

> Brave men were living before Agamemnon.

See *Carm.* 4. 9. 25:

> Vixere fortes ante Agamemnona.

(32)   From *Don Juan* 3. 98:

> We learn from Horace, 'Homer sometimes sleeps.'

See *Ars Poet.* 359:

> Quandoque bonus dormitat Homerus.

(33)   Again in *Don Juan* (5. 159) we have the same expression:

> Meanwhile, as Homer sometimes sleeps, perhaps
> You'll pardon to my muse a few short naps.

(34)   From *Ode on Venice*, stanza 4:

> Those whose red right hands have bought
> Rights cheaply earned with blood.

See *Carm.* 1. 2. 2-3: *rubente dextera.*

(35)   From *Childe Harold's Pilgrimage* 4. 174:

> Where yon bar
> Of girdling mountains intercepts the sight
> The Sabine farm was tilled, the weary Bard's delight.

Horace frequently refers to his Sabine farm, the gift of Maecenas. See *Carm.* 2. 16. 37, 2. 18. 14, 3. 1. 47, *Serm.* 2. 7. 118, *Epist.* 1. 14. 1, 1. 16. 1 ff.

(36)   From *Don Juan* 2. 205:

> Oh, Love! of whom great Caesar was the suitor,
>   Titus the master, Antony the slave,
> Horace, Catullus, scholars.

(37)   From *The Age of Bronze*, stanza 12:

> Why wouldst thou leave calm Hartwell's green abode,
> Apician table, and Horatian ode?

(38)   From *Farewell Petition to J. C. H., Esqre.*:

> Tell him, that not in vain I shall assay
> To tread and trace our 'old Horatian way,' [1]
> And be (with prose supply my dearth of rhymes)
> What better men have been in better times.

(39)   In the preface to *The Prophecy of Dante*, Byron says:

> 'In adopting this plan I have had in my mind the Cassandra of Lycophron, and the Prophecy of Nereus by Horace, as well as the Prophecies of Holy Writ.'

For the Horatian reference see *Carm.* 1. 15.

---

[1] See Roscommon, *An Essay on Translated Verse*, l. 2.

(40)   From a letter to William Gifford, November 12, 1813:

'It deserves no better than the first, as the work of a week, and scribbled *stans pede in uno* (by the by, the only foot I have to stand on).'

See *Serm.* 1. 4. 10.

(41)   From Byron's journal, November 22, 1813:

'Oh that face!—by *te, diva potens Cypri*, I would, to be beloved by that woman, build and burn another Troy.'

See *Carm.* 1. 3. 1.

(42)   From Byron's journal, November, 1813:

'I thought, if crushed, he would have fallen, when *fractus illabitur orbis.*'

See *Carm.* 3. 3. 7: *fractus illabatur orbis.*

(43)   From Byron's journal, February 18, 1814:

'Divesne prisco natus ab Inacho
Nil interest an pauper et infima
De gente, sub dio [*sic*] moreris,
Victima nil miserantis Orci.
Omnes eodem cogimur, etc.

'Is there anything beyond?—*who* knows?
He that can't tell.'

See *Carm.* 2. 3. 21 ff.   (For *dio* read *divo.*)

(44)   From a letter to Thomas Moore, March 3, 1814:

'Even Horace's *Nonum prematur* must have been intended for the Millennium, or some longer-lived generation than ours. I wonder how much we should have had of *him*, had he observed his own doctrines to the letter.'

See *Ars Poet.* 388.

(45)   From a letter to Thomas Moore, February 2, 1815:

'I wish you would respond, for I am here *oblitusque meorum obliviscendus et illis.*'

See *Epist.* 1. 11. 9.

(46)   From a letter to Thomas Moore, June 1, 1818:

'Failure will be probable, and my fair woman, *superne*, end in a fish.'

See *Ars Poet.* 3-4:

Ut turpiter atrum
Desinat in piscem mulier formosa superne.

(47)   From a letter to John Murray, May 25, 1819:

'You may omit the *note* of reference to Hobhouse's travels in
Canto second [of *Don Juan*], and you will put as motto to the whole:
Difficile est proprie communia dicere.
Horace.'

See *Ars Poet*. 128.

(48)   From Byron's diary, January 21, 1821:

'It is three minutes past twelve.—" 'Tis the middle of the night by
the castle clock," and I am now thirty-three!
Eheu fugaces, Postume, Postume,
Labuntur anni.'

See *Carm*. 2. 14. 1-2.

(49)   From a letter to John Murray, July 11, 1821:

'However little this poem [*Hints from Horace*] may resemble the
annexed Latin, it has been submitted to one of the great rules of
Horace, having been kept in the desk for more than *nine* years.'

See *Ars Poet*. 388.

(50)   From the first letter to John Murray 'on the Rev. W. L.
Bowles' Strictures on the Life and Writings of Pope:'

'You say that a "fountain is as clear or clearer than *glass*," to
express its beauty:
O fons Bandusiae, splendidior vitro.'

See *Carm*. 3. 13. 1.

(51)   From a letter to Thomas Moore, March 8, 1822:

'A request from you and Hobhouse would have come upon me like
two out of the *tribus Anticyris*—with which, however, Horace despairs
of purging a poet.'

See *Ars Poet*. 299-302:

Nanciscetur enim pretium nomenque poetae,
Si tribus Anticyris caput insanabile numquam
Tonsori Licino commiserit.   O ego laevus,
Qui purgor bilem sub verni temporis horam!

(52)   From *Don Juan* 3. 81:

But *he* had genius—when a turncoat has it,
    The *Vates irritabilis* takes care
That without notice few full moons shall pass it.

See *Epist*. 2. 2. 102: *genus irritabile vatum*.

II. Probable traces of Horace

(1)   From *Cain* 2. 1. 71-72:

> Thou canst not
> *All* die.

See *Carm*. 3. 30. 6:

> Non omnis moriar.

(2)   From *Childe Harold's Pilgrimage* 3. 73:

> On delighted wing
> Spurning the clay-cold bonds which round our being cling.

See *Carm*. 3. 2. 23-24:

> Udam
> Spernit humum fugiente penna.

(3)   From *Childe Harold's Pilgrimage* 4. 125:

> Circumstance, that unspiritual God
> And Miscreator, makes and helps along
> Our coming evils with a crutch-like rod.

Mr. E. H. Coleridge has the following note on this passage:

> 'Circumstance is personified as halting Nemesis—
> Pede poena claudo.
>   (*Carm*. 3. 2. 32.)'

(4)   From *The Bride of Abydos* 1. 11:

> Think'st thou that I could bear to part
> With thee, and learn to halve my heart?
> .   .   .   .
> Years have not seen, Time shall not see,
> The hour that tears my soul from thee:
> Even Azrael, from his deadly quiver
>   When flies that shaft, and fly it must,
> That parts all else, shall doom for ever
>   Our hearts to undivided dust.

See *Carm*. 2. 17. 5-12:

> A, te meae si partem animae rapit
> Maturior vis, quid moror altera,
>   Nec carus aeque nec superstes
>   Integer?   Ille dies utramque
> Ducet ruinam.   Non ego perfidum
> Dixi sacramentum: ibimus, ibimus,
>   Utcumque praecedes, supremum
>   Carpere iter comites parati.

(5)   The same idea is found in *Stanzas to Jessy*, stanza 1:

> There is a mystic thread of life
> So dearly wreath'd with mine alone,
> That Destiny's relentless knife
> At once must sever both, or none.

(6)   From *The Curse of Minerva*, ll. 289-290:

> The hero bounding at his country's call,
> The glorious death that consecrates his fall.

See *Carm.* 3. 2. 13:

> Dulce et decorum est pro patria mori.

(7)   From *The Bride of Abydos* 2. 2:

> That field with blood bedewed in vain,
> The desert of old Priam's pride;
> The tombs, sole relics of his reign.

See *Carm.* 2. 1. 29-32:

> Quis non Latino sanguine pinguior
> Campus sepulcris impia proelia
> Testatur auditumque Medis
> Hesperiae sonitum ruinae?

(8)   From *Childe Harold's Pilgrimage* 2. 8:

> Sophists, madly vain of dubious lore.

See *Carm.* 1. 34. 2-3:

> Insanientis dum sapientiae
> Consultus erro.

(9)   From *The Two Foscari* 4. 1. 129-130:

> To lash up from the deep the Adrian waves,
> And waken Auster, sovereign of the tempest.

See *Carm.* 3. 3. 4-5:

> Auster,
> Dux inquieti turbidus Hadriae.

Also *Carm.* 4. 14. 20-21:

> Indomitas prope qualis undas
> Exercet Auster.

(10)   From *Childe Harold's Pilgrimage* 2. 39:

> Dark Sappho! could not Verse immortal save
> That breast imbued with such immortal fire?
> Could she not live who life eternal gave?

See *Carm.* 4. 9. 10-12:

> Spirat adhuc amor
> Vivuntque commissi calores
> Aeoliae fidibus puellae.

(11)   From *Don Juan* 15. 8:

> O death! thou dunnest of all duns! thou daily
> Knockest at doors, at first with modest tap,
> Like a meek tradesman when approaching palely
> Some splendid debtor he would take by sap:
> But oft denied, as Patience 'gins to fail, he
> Advances with exasperated rap.

See *Carm.* 1. 4. 13-14:

> Pallida mors aequo pulsat pede pauperum tabernas
> Regumque turris.

(12)   Sub-title to *The Age of Bronze*:

> *Carmen Seculare et Annus Haud Mirabilis.*

The first part of this is probably an echo of Horace's *Carmen Saeculare.*

PERCY BYSSHE SHELLEY

I. *A Paraphrase Attributed to Shelley*

In the discussion of the influence of Horace upon Shelley, first place must be given to an anonymous paraphrase of *Carm. 3. 19* which Mr. H. Buxton Forman concludes to be a genuine Shelleyan production, and which he prints in the appendix to his library edition of Shelley's poems. I quote his argument in favor of the paraphrase:[1]

'The story of this paraphrase, not hitherto known as a work of Shelley's, is somewhat complicated. Among the Leigh Hunt MSS. placed at my disposal by Mr. S. R. Townshend Mayer, are two sheets of extremely thin foreign paper such as numerous poems of Shelley's were written upon for convenience of transit through the post, on which sheets, in Mrs. Shelley's writing, are this paraphrase from Horace, and *The Magic Horse*, from Christofano Bronzino. The sheets have been folded in three as they would be if enclosed in a letter. Had this been all that was known of the MS., I should scarcely have hesitated, looking at the internal evidence, and considering that the paper was found among other transcripts of Shelley's works by his wife, to have attributed the translations positively to him; and I do not, in fact, doubt that they are his. But in a periodical of Leigh Hunt's, *The Companion*, for the 26th of March, 1828 (the number, as originally printed), this paraphrase from Horace appears, without any translator's name. If there were any intrinsic quality in this poem to countenance for a moment the supposition that it came from Hunt's pen—and I do not think there is,— such a notion would be disposed of by the fact that when he printed *The Companion* as a book, he omitted this piece, and that he did not print it among his translations, admirable as it is. In the weekly number of *The Companion* following that which contains this paraphrase, he apologizes, on the plea of illness, for using something of Procter's, sent to him "for another purpose"; and the presumption is that he used a translation of Shelley's under like circumstances. Following the search further, Mr. Mayer and I discovered Leigh Hunt's own copy of this paraphrase—"copy" that has evidently been used to print from. The ode has there been introduced as the first of a series of articles to be called *The Dessert* and to consist of compositions "not large enough to stand by themselves"; and this introduction, which after all did not appear with the ode, concludes with the words, "Here have we been going to heaven, when our sole design was to introduce a thing no less earthly than one of Horace's odes. But if ever heaven and earth meet (not to speak it profanely), it is at the table of a wit and good fellows; and so, finding ourselves right in that matter, we call upon Horace for his ode." After the last line of the ode, Hunt has written, "The

[1] Shelley's *Poetical Works*, ed. Forman, 4. 540 (note).

following is a portrait from the life, and comes well after our dinner-party.   The subject is not a *beau ideal*, like Telephus; but he is human and Horatian, and might illustrate a series of odes, from the *mox reficit rates* of the beginning, to the *est mihi nonum* of Book the fourth.'' Then follows the heading, "Sketches from the Club-Book—No. 1. Old Charlton," such being the title of the composition of Procter's used with the apology already referred to.   It is to be noted further that, whereas in Mrs. Shelley's transcript we read, *I have given myself up to the spirit of the occasion*, in the argument as published by Hunt we read, *The translator has given himself up*, etc.   The word *somewhere*, after *dinner party*, is omitted in Hunt's copy, where we also read, after *enjoyment*, the words *drinking their toasts and discussing their mistresses*.   He inserts further, before the word *Commentators*, the following: *His proposal to torment the old fellow next door, who envies them their good humor, is very pleasant*.   I should say from the writing that this translation belongs to about the year 1820.'

Subsequently Mr. Forman remarks:[1]

'I have already said that the handwriting of Mrs. Shelley in this MS. seems to be of about the year 1820; and it may be added that the playful style of both pieces [viz., the paraphrase of Horace and the translation from Bronzino] corresponds with the treatment of the *Hymn to Mercury* and *The Witch of Atlas*—both compositions of 1820.'

The ode in question (3. 19) runs as follows:

> Quantum distet ab Inacho
>   Codrus pro patria non timidus mori
> Narras et genus Aeaci
>   Et pugnata sacro bella sub Ilio;
> Quo Chium pretio cadum
>   Mercemur, quis aquam temperet ignibus,
> Quo praebente domum et quota
>   Paelignis caream frigoribus, taces.
> Da lunae propere novae,
>   Da noctis mediae, da, puer, auguris
> Murenae: tribus aut novem
>   Miscentur cyathis pocula commodis.
> Qui Musas amat imparis,
>   Ternos ter cyathos attonitus petet
> Vates; tris prohibet supra
>   Rixarum metuens tangere Gratia
> Nudis iuncta sororibus.
>   Insanire iuvat: cur Berecyntiae
> Cessant flamina tibiae?
>   Cur pendet tacita fistula cum lyra?

[1]Shelley's *Poetical Works*, ed. Forman, 4. 542 (note).

Parcentis ego dexteras
  Odi: sparge rosas; audiat invidus
Dementem strepitum Lycus
  Et vicina seni non habilis Lyco.
Spissa te nitidum coma,
  Puro te similem, Telephe, Vespero
Tempestiva petit Rhode;
  Me lentus Glycerae torret amor meae.

The paraphrase:

THE DINNER PARTY ANTICIPATED

Argument.—The Poet rallies his young friend Telephus upon his fondness for talking of genealogy and antiquities, and complains that he does not fix a day for having a dinner-party somewhere. The thought of such a meeting fires his imagination, and he supposes them all in the midst of their enjoyment, and talking of their mistresses. Commentators differ, as usual, upon passages in this ode. I have given myself up to the spirit of the occasion, as the most likely, if not the most learned, guide.

Dear Telephus, you trace divinely
The Grecian king who died so finely;
And show a zeal that betters us,
For all the house of Aeacus;
And make us to our special joy,
Feel every blow bestowed at Troy:
But not a syllable do you say,
Of where we are to dine some day;
Not one about a little stock
Of neat, you rogue; nor what o'clock
Some four of us may come together,
And shut the cold out this strange weather.

Good Gods! I feel it done already!
More wine, my boy! There—steady, steady:
'Whose health?' whose health! why here's the moon:
She's young: may she be older soon:
'Whose next?' Why next, I think, it's clear
Comes Mother Midnight—Here's to her:
And after her, with three at least,
Our reverend friend the new-made priest.
Three cups in one then. *Three* and *we!*
Fill, as is fitting, three times three:
For poets in their moods divine
Measure their goblets by the Nine;
Although the Graces, naked tremblers!
Talk of a third to common tumblers.

Parties like us, true souls and glad,
Have right and title to be mad.
Who told the flutes there to leave off?
They've not been breathed yet half enough:
And who hung up the pipes and lyres?
They have not done with half our fires.
The roses too—heap, heap one's hair!
I hate a right hand that can spare.
Let the old envious dog next door,
Old Lycus, hear the maddening roar,
And the blithe girl (she'll love it well)
Whom Lycus finds—not haveable.

Ah! Telephus! those locks of thine,
That lie so thick, and smooth, and shine,
And that complete and sparkling air,
That gilds one's evenings like a star,
'Tis these for which the hussy wishes,
And comes to meet with willing blushes.
'And you too, Horace, what fair she
Inspires you now?' Oh, as for me,
I'm in my old tormenting way—
Burnt at a slow fire, day by day,
For my dull dear Glycera.[1]

II. *Unquestionable traces of Horace*

(1)   Motto of *Zastrozzi*, chapter 17:

Si fractus illabatur orbis,
Impavidum ferient ruinae.

See *Carm.* 3. 3. 7-8.   Horace.

(2)   Note on *Queen Mab* 8. 211-212:

'Again, so general was this opinion [viz., that mankind was free
from all suffering before the theft of fire by Prometheus] that Horace,
a poet of the Augustan age, writes:

Audax omnia perpeti,
Gens humana ruit per vetitum nefas;
Audax Iapeti genus
Ignem fraude mala gentibus intulit:
Post ignem aetheria domo
Subductum, macies et nova febrium
Terris incubuit cohors,
Semotique prius tarda necessitas
Lethi corripuit gradum.'

See *Carm.* 1. 3. 25-33.   (For *lethi* in l. 33 read *leti.*)

---

[1] A detailed and careful comparison between the ode and the paraphrase will be found in *Percy
Bysshe Shelley's Sprach-Studien: seine Uebersetzungen aus dem Lateinischen und Griechischen*, by Florian
Asanger, pp. 57 ff.

(3) Note on *Queen Mab* 5. 93-94:

'The nobleman who employs the peasants of his neighborhood in building his palaces until *iam pauca aratro iugera regiae moles relinquunt* flatters himself that he has gained the title of a patriot by yielding to the impulses of vanity.'

See *Carm.* 2. 15. 1-2. (For *relinquunt* read *relinquent*; but Shelley may have made the change intentionally.)

(4) Advertisement to *Oedipus Tyrannus, or Swellfoot the Tyrant*:

'The tenderness with which he [the supposititious author] treats the PIGS proves him to have been . . . possibly *Epicuri de grege porcus*.'

See *Epist.* 1. 4. 16: *Epicuri de grege porcum.*

(5) From *A Defense of Poetry*:

'These things are not the less poetry *quia carent vate sacro*.'

See *Carm.* 4. 9. 28: *carent quia vate sacro.*

(6) From a letter to William Godwin, July 29, 1812:

'Did Greek and Roman literature refine the soul of Johnson? Does it extend the views of the thousand narrow bigots educated in the very bosom of classicality? But

in publica commoda peccem,
Si longo sermone morer tua tempora,

says Horace at the commencement of his longest letter.'

See *Epist.* 2. 1. 3-4.

(7) The first seven words of the foregoing quotation are again used at the end of a letter to Thomas Love Peacock, November, 1820.

(8) From a letter to Thomas Love Peacock, January 26, 1819:

'You see how ill I follow the maxim of Horace, at least in its literal sense: *nil admirari*—which I should say, *prope res est una*—to prevent there ever being anything admirable in the world.'

See *Epist.* 1. 6. 1.

(9) *Nil admirari* is again quoted in a letter to John Gisborne, June 18, 1822.

(10) From a letter to Thomas Jefferson Hogg, November 26, 1813:

'Do not persevere in writing after you grow weary of your toil; *aliquando bonus dormitat Homerus*.'

See *Ars Poet.* 359. (For *aliquando* read *quandoque*.)

(11)   From a letter to 'a person in London,' August 18, 1812:

> 'Indeed, a poem is safe; an iron-souled prosecutor would scarcely dare to attack *genus irritabile vatum*.'

See *Epist.* 2. 2. 102.

(12)   From a fragmentary poem beginning, 'Alas! this is not what I thought life was,' ll. 7-8:

> With triple brass
> Of calm endurance my weak breast I armed.

See *Carm.* 1. 3. 9-10:

> Aes triplex
> Circa pectus erat.

(13)   From *Queen Mab* 9. 57:

> Mild was the slow necessity of death.

See *Carm.* 1. 3. 32-33:

> Tarda necessitas
> Leti.

(Shelley, it will be recalled, quotes this phrase from Horace in his notes to *Queen Mab*. See above, p. 84.)

III.   *Probable traces of Horace*

(1)   From *Peter Bell the Third*, l. 538:

> Ex luce praebens fumum.

See *Ars Poet.* 143:

> Non fumum ex fulgore, sed ex fumo dare lucem.

(2)   From *Queen Mab* 5. 171-176:

> . . . Him of resolute and unchanging will;
> Whom, nor the plaudits of a servile crowd,
> Nor the vile joys of tainting luxury,
> Can bribe to yield his elevated soul
> To Tyranny or Falsehood, though they wield
> With blood-red hand the scepter of the world.

See *Carm.* 3. 3. 1-6:

> Iustum et tenacem propositi virum
> Non civium ardor prava iubentium,
> Non voltus instantis tyranni
> Mente quatit solida, neque Auster,
> Dux inquieti turbidus Hadriae,
> Nec fulminantis magna manus Iovis.

For 'blood-red hand' see *Carm.* 1. 2. 2-3: *rubente dextera*.

(3) From *The Revolt of Islam*, ll. 3165-3166:

> As if the world's wide continent
> Had fallen in universal ruin wracked.

See *Carm.* 3. 3. 7-8:

> Si fractus illabatur orbis,
> Impavidum ferient ruinae.

(Shelley quotes this at the beginning of *Zastrozzi*, chapter 17; see above, p. 84.)

(4) From *The Revolt of Islam*, ll. 3529-3531:

> Wisdom, ...
> . . . . and tameless scorn of ill,
> Thrice steeped in molten steel the unconquerable will.

This seems to contain traces of two familiar Horatian themes—the *aes triplex* of *Carm.* 1. 3. 9, and the *tenacem propositi virum*, etc., of *Carm.* 3. 3. 1 ff.

(5) From *The Revolt of Islam*, ll. 3746-3747:

> And fame, in human hope which sculptured was,
> Survive the perished scrolls of unenduring brass.

See *Carm.* 3. 30. 1:

> Exegi monumentum aere perennius.

(6) From *Adonais*, ll. 264-266:

> Whose fame
> Over his living head like Heaven is bent,
> An early but enduring monument.

Compare the preceding quotation from Horace. The idea of the eternity of fame is, of course, common to many poets; but the use of the phrase 'enduring monument' points to a Horatian origin.

(7) From *Prometheus Unbound* 2. 4. 49-52:

> On the race of man
> First famine, and then toil, and then disease,
> Strife, wounds, and ghastly death unseen before,
> Fell.

See *Carm.* 1. 3. 29-33:

> Post ignem aetheria domo
> Subductum macies et nova febrium
> Terris incubuit cohors,
> Semotique prius tarda necessitas
> Leti corripuit gradum.

(It will be remembered that Shelley was familiar with this ode; see pp. 84, 86.)

(8)   From *Prometheus Unbound* 3. 1. 50-51:

> The earthquake of his chariot thundering up
> Olympus.

See *Carm.* 1. 12. 58:

> Tu gravi curru quaties Olympum.

(9)   From *Adonais*, l. 3:

> Thaw not the frost which binds so dear a head.

See *Carm.* 1. 24. 1-2:

> Quis desiderio sit pudor aut modus
> Tam cari capitis?

Horace's ode is a lament for Quintilius, as Shelley's poem is an elegy on Keats.

(10)   From *Adonais*, l. 188:

> Evening must usher night, night urge the morrow.

Compare with this use of 'urge' *Epod.* 17. 25:

> Urget diem nox et dies noctem.

(11)   From *Charles the First* 2. 2. 117-118:

> The Spirit of the Time,
> Which spurs to rage the many-headed beast [the populace].

See *Epist.* 1. 1. 76:

> Belua multorum es [i. e., popule Romane] capitum.

It must be acknowledged, however, that this bit of Horace has been so often used as to be a commonplace.

(12)   From *Ode to Liberty*, l. 258:

> Beckons the Sun from the Eoan wave.

See *Epod.* 2. 51:

> Eois . . . fluctibus.

(13)   From *Oedipus Tyrannus, or Swellfoot the Tyrant* 2. 2. 22-27:

> Allow me now to recommend this dish—
> A simple kickshaw by your Persian cook,
> Such as is served at the great King's second table.
> The price and pains which its ingredients cost
> Might have maintained some dozen families
> A winter or two.

The 'Persian cook,' one of the evidences of luxury and extravagance, recalls *Carm.* 1. 38. 1:

> Persicos odi, puer, apparatus.

JOHN KEATS

I. *Unquestionable traces of Horace*

Nowhere in the poems of Keats can there be found a direct quotation or even a definite echo from Horace. There are, however, a few reminiscences in his letters, which I append.

(1)   From a letter to B. R. Haydon (probably of December, 1818):

> 'I will be with you to-morrow morning and stop all day—we will hate the profane vulgar and make us wings.'

See *Carm.* 3. 1. 1:

> Odi profanum volgus.

(2)   From a letter to Thomas Keats, July 11, 1818:

> 'As to the *profanum vulgus*, I must incline to the Scotch.'

See the foregoing citation from Horace.

(3)   From a letter to Richard Woodhouse, October 27, 1818:

> 'Your letter gave me great satisfaction, more on account of its friendliness than any relish of that matter in it which is accounted so acceptable in the *genus irritabile*.'

See *Epist.* 2. 2. 102:

> Genus irritabile vatum.

II.   *Probable traces of Horace*

(1)   From a letter to George and Georgiana Keats, December, 1818:

> 'I am in daily expectation of letters—*Nil desperandum.*'

The quotation may be found in Horace (*Carm.* 1. 7. 27); but it is so very familiar a catchword that one cannot feel positive of its precise derivation.

(2)   From *The Cap and Bells* 61. 3-5:

> 'Behold, your Majesty, upon the brow
> Of yonder hill, what crowds of people!'   'Whew!
> The monster's always after something new.'

The use of *monster* to describe the populace recalls Horace's *belua multorum capitum* (*Epist.* 1. 1. 76); but see above, reference to Shelley's probable use of the same passage, p. 88.

ALFRED LORD TENNYSON

I. *Unquestionable traces of Horace*

(1) As we have seen, Tennyson's acquaintance with Horace began early in his life; and it is appropriate that we should find in his first extant letter, written to his aunt, Marianne Fytche, when he was twelve years old, the following sentence:

> 'It [the word *diffused* in *Samson Agonistes*] has the same meaning as "temere" in one of the Odes of Horace, Book the second:
>
> > Sic temere et rosa
> > Canos odorati capillos,
>
> of which this is a free translation: "Why lie we not at random, under the shade of the plantain (*sub platano*), having our hoary head perfumed with rose water?" '

See *Carm.* 2. 11. 14-15.

(2) Motto of *Parnassus:*

> Exegi monumentum . . . . . .
> Quod non . . . .
> Possit diruere . . . innumerabilis
> Annorum series et fuga temporum.
> > > Horace.

See *Carm.* 3. 30. 1-5. Tennyson's poem shows no trace of the Horatian ode, however, unless it be the phrase 'flight of the Ages' (*fuga temporum*).

(3) From *Becket* 5. 2:

> And one [wife] an *uxor pauperis Ibyci.*

See *Carm.* 3. 15. 1.

(4) From an undated letter to James Spedding:

> 'The birds must sing and the furze bloom for you and Fitzgerald alone, *par nobile fratrum.*'

See *Serm.* 2. 3. 243.

(5) From a letter-diary written from Glastonbury, August, 1854:

> 'I took shelter over Arimathaean Joseph's bones in the crypt of his chapel, for they say (*credat Iudaeus*) he lies there.'

See *Serm.* 1. 5. 100.

(6)   From *A Dream of Fair Women* [Cleopatra]:

> I died a Queen.

Tennyson's note on the line:

> 'Cf. *Non humilis mulier.   (Carm. 1. 37. 32.)*'

(7)   From *Epilogue:*

> For dare we dally with the sphere
>   As he did half in jest,
> Old Horace?   'I will strike' said he
>   'The stars with head sublime.'

See *Carm.* 1. 1. 36:

> Sublimi feriam sidera vertice.

(8)   From *Poets and their Bibliographies*:

> And you, old popular Horace, you the wise
> Adviser of the nine-years-ponder'd lay.

See *Ars Poet.* 386-388:

> > > Siquid tamen olim
> Scripseris . . . .
> . . . . . nonum . . prematur in annum.

(9)   From *Becket* 1. 1:

> The included Danaë has escaped again
> Her tower, and her Acrisius.

See *Carm.* 3. 16. 1, 3, 5-7:

> Inclusam Danaen turris aenea
> . . . . . . munierant satis,
> . . . .
> Si non Acrisium virginis abditae
> Custodem pavidum Iuppiter et Venus
> Risissent.

(10)   From *Lucretius*:

> No larger feast than under plane or pine
> With neighbors laid along the grass, to take
> Only such cups as left us friendly-warm.

See *Carm.* 2. 11. 13, 14, 17:

> Cur non sub alta vel platano vel hac
> Pinu iacentes . . . .
> Potamus?

Tennyson's whole poem is, naturally enough, saturated with Lucretius, who also has 'neighbors laid along the grass' (2. 29); but 'under plane or pine' is clearly Horatian.   The reminiscence carries us back to the boyish exegesis of the same passage, noticed above (No. 1).

(11)   From *The Two Voices*:

> Soil'd with noble dust.

See *Carm.* 2. 1. 22:

> Non indecoro pulvere sordidos.

(12)   The same phrase is found in *The Vale of Bones:*

> Your brows with noble dust defil'd,

with a reference to the Horatian ode in a footnote.

(13)   Motto of the same poem:

> Albis informem . . . ossibus agrum.
>   Horace.

See *Serm.* 1. 8. 16.

(14)   Motto of the poem beginning, 'Did not thy roseate lips outvie':

> Ulla si iuris tibi peierati
> Poena, Barine, nocuisset umquam,
> Dente si nigro fieres vel uno
>   Turpior ungui,
> Crederem.
>   Horace.

See *Carm.* 2. 8. 1-5.

(15)   From *A Dream of Fair Women*:

> Saw God divide the night with flying flame.

See *Carm.* 1. 34. 5-6:

> Diespiter
> Igni corusco nubila dividens.

Hallam Tennyson notes this parallel (Eversley edition).

(16)   From *In Memoriam* 127:

> The brute earth lightens to the sky.

See *Carm.* 1. 34. 9:

> Bruta tellus.

Noted by Hallam Tennyson.

(17)   To a translation made by Hallam Tennyson of *Carm.* 1. 38

his father contributed these lines:

> Dream not of where some sunny rose may linger
> > Later in autumn.

See ll. 3-4:

> Mitte sectari, rosa quo locorum
> > Sera moretur.

II. *Probable traces of Horace*

(1) From *Will:*

> O well for him whose will is strong!
> He suffers, but he will not suffer long;
> He suffers, but he cannot suffer wrong:
> For him nor moves the loud world's random mock,
> Nor all Calamity's hugest waves confound,
> Who seems a promontory of rock,
> That, compass'd round with turbulent sound,
> In middle ocean meets the surging shock,
> Tempest-buffeted, citadel-crown'd.

See *Carm. 3. 3.* 1-8:

> Iustum et tenacem propositi virum
> Non civium ardor prava iubentium,
> > Non voltus instantis tyranni
> > > Mente quatit solida, neque Auster,
> Dux inquieti turbidus Hadriae,
> > Nec fulminantis magna manus Iovis;
> > > Si fractus illabatur orbis,
> > > > Impavidum ferient ruinae.

(2) From *Tiresias:*

> No sound is breathed so potent to coerce,
> And to conciliate, as their names who dare
> For that sweet mother land which gave them birth
> Nobly to do, nobly to die.

See *Carm. 3. 2. 13:*

> Dulce et decorum est pro patria mori;

Carm. 3. 19. 2:

> Pro patria non timidus mori;

Carm. 4. 9. 51-52:

> Non ille pro caris amicis
> Aut patria timidus perire.

(3)   From *In Memoriam* 89:

> The dust and din and steam of town.

See *Carm.* 3. 29. 12:

> Fumum et opes strepitumque Romae.

(4)   There is a similar phrase in *To the Rev. F. D. Maurice:*

> Far from noise and smoke of town.

(5)   From *Edwin Morris:*

> Finish'd to the finger nail.

See *Serm.* 1. 5. 32-33:

> Ad unguem
> Factus homo.

(6)   From *Ode on the Death of the Duke of Wellington :*

> Whole in himself.

See *Serm.* 2. 7. 86:

> In se ipso totus.

(7)   From *The Lover's Tale* 1:

> Death drew nigh and beat the doors of Life.

See *Carm.* 1. 4. 13:

> Pallida mors aequo pulsat pede pauperum tabernas.

(8)   From *The Princess* 1:

> We remember love ourselves
> In our sweet youth.

See *Carm.* 1. 16. 22-24:

> Me quoque pectoris
> Temptavit in dulci iuventa
> Fervor.

(9)   From *Morte D'Arthur:*

> The giddy pleasure of the eyes.

See *Epist.* 2. 1. 188:

> Incertos oculos et gaudia vana.

(10)   From *In Memoriam* 84:

> Thy spirit should fail from off the globe,
> What time mine own might also flee,
>   As link'd with thine in love and fate,
>   And, hovering o'er the dolorous strait
> To the other shore, involved in thee,

> Arrive at last the blessed goal,
>   And He that died in Holy Land
> Would reach us out the shining hand,
>   And take us as a single soul.

See *Carm.* 2. 17. 5 ff.:

> A, te meae si partem animae rapit
> Maturior vis, quid moror altera,
>   Nec carus aeque nec superstes
>   Integer? Ille dies utramque
> Ducet ruinam. Non ego perfidum
> Dixi sacramentum: ibimus, ibimus,
>   Utcumque praecedes, supremum
>   Carpere iter comites parati.

(11) From *The Lotos-Eaters:*

> To live and lie reclined
> On the hills like Gods together, careless of mankind.

Hallam Tennyson refers to *Serm.* 1. 5. 101:

> Namque deos didici securum agere aevum.

Also to Lucretius 5. 83, 6. 58:

> Nam bene qui didicere deos securum agere aevum.

Horace's line is clearly an echo of Lucretius. It is impossible to say which Tennyson had in mind.

(12) From *In Memoriam* 1:

> To dance with death, to beat the ground.

See *Carm.* 1. 37. 1-2:

> Nunc est bibendum, nunc pede libero
> Pulsanda tellus;

and *Carm.* 1. 4. 7:

> Alterno terram quatiunt pede.

(13) From *In Memoriam* 115:

> Now fades the last long streak of snow,
>   Now burgeons every maze of quick
>   About the flowering squares, and thick
> By ashen roots the violets blow.

See *Carm.* 4. 7. 1-2:

> Diffugere nives, redeunt iam gramina campis
> Arboribusque comae.

(14) From *In Memoriam* 107:
>   Fiercely flies
> The blast of North and East, and ice
> Makes daggers at the sharpen'd eaves.
>   . . . .
>   But fetch the wine,
> Arrange the board and brim the glass;
>
> Bring in great logs and let them lie,
> To make a solid core of heat.

See *Carm*. 1. 9. 1-8:
> Vides ut alta stet nive candidum
> Soracte, nec iam sustineant onus
>   Silvae laborantes, geluque
>   Flumina constiterint acuto.
> Dissolve frigus ligna super foco
> Large reponens atque benignius
>   Deprome quadrimum Sabina,
>   O Thaliarche, merum diota.

(15) From *In Memoriam* 89:
> And break the livelong summer day
> With banquet in the distant woods.

See *Carm*. 2. 7. 6-7:
> Cum quo morantem saepe diem mero
>   Fregi.

(16) From *Supposed Confessions of a Second-Rate Sensitive Mind:*
> To arm in proof, and guard about
> With triple-mailèd trust.

This is clearly an echo of Horace's *aes triplex* (*Carm*. 1. 3. 9); but the idea has become so familiar that one cannot say whether the particular instance is a direct reminiscence, or comes through an intermediary.

(17) From *Morte D'Arthur:*
> Till on to dawn, when dreams
> Begin to feel the truth and stir of day.

See *Serm*. 1. 10. 33:
> Post mediam noctem, . . . cum somnia vera.

(18) From *To ———, after Reading a Life and Letters:*
> Keep nothing sacred: 'tis but just
> The many-headed beast should know.

See *Epist.* 1. 1. 76:

> Belua multorum es capitum.

The similarity is unmistakable; but, as before (p. 88), the phrase is almost a commonplace.

(19)   From *The Princess* 1:

> Whate'er my grief to find her less than fame.

See *Epist.* 1. 11. 3:

> Maiora minorave fama.

(20)   From *Locksley Hall:*

> Great Orion sloping slowly to the West.

See *Carm.* 3. 27. 18:

> Pronus Orion.

(The first meaning of *pronus* is 'inclined forward'.)

(21)   From *The Marriage of Geraint:*

> On either shining shoulder laid a hand

See *Carm.* 2. 5. 18:

> Albo sic umero nitens.

(22)   From *Beautiful City:*

> The tides of a civic insanity.

See *Carm.* 3. 24. 26:

> Rabiem . . . . civicam.

(23)   From *The Two Voices:*

> The joy that mixes man with Heaven

See *Carm.* 1. 1. 29-30:

> Me doctarum hederae praemia frontium
> Dis miscent superis.

(24)   From *The Cup* 1. 1:

> No rushing on the game—the net—the net

Hallam Tennyson gives a reference to *Carm.* 1. 1. 28:

> Seu rupit teretes Marsus aper plagas

(25)   From *In Memoriam* 115:

> The happy birds that change their sky

See *Epist.* 1. 11. 27: *caelum, non animum mutant.*

ROBERT BROWNING

I. Unquestionable traces of Horace

(1)   From *The Inn Album* 7:

> But *ne trucidet coram populo*
> *Iuvenis senem!*   Right the Horatian rule!

See *Ars Poet.* 185:

> Ne pueros coram populo Medea trucidet.

Here, as frequently, Browning alters the Horatian line to fit the situation.

(2)   From *Pacchiarotto*, stanza 16:

> The paraphrase—which I much need—is
> From Horace—*per ignes incedis.*

See *Carm.* 2. 1. 7: *incedis per ignis.*

(3)   The title of the poem *Instans Tyrannus* comes from *Carm.* 3. 3. 3: *instantis tyranni.*

(4)   From *The Statue and the Bust:*

> How strive you?   *De te fabula!*

See *Serm.* 1. 1. 69-70.

(5)   From *Parleyings with Certain People of Importance* (*Parleyings with George Bubb Dodington*, stanza 6):

> In armor, true *aes triplex*, breast and back
> Binding about.

See *Carm.* 1. 3. 9-10:

> Aes triplex
> Circa pectus erat.

(6)   In the same section of the same poem we read:

> Triply cased in brass—

a reference, of course, to the same Horatian phrase.

(7)   From *The Two Poets of Croisic*, stanza 75:

> Irritabilis gens.

See *Epist.* 2. 2. 102:

> Genus irritabile vatum.

(8)   From *The Two Poets of Croisic*, stanza 75:

> Leisurely works mark the *divinior mens.*

See *Serm.* 1. 4. 43:

> Mens divinior.

(9)   The same phrase is found in the same poem, l. 38:

> All his day's *divinior mens.*

(10)   From *The Ring and the Book* 8:

> *Ne sit*
> *Marita quae rotundioribus*
> *Onusta mammis* . . . *baccis ambulet:*
> Her bosom shall display the big round balls,
> No braver proudly borne by wedded wife!
> With which Horatian promise I conclude.

See *Epod.* 8. 13-14:

> Nec sit marita, quae rotundioribus
> Onusta bacis ambulet.

(11)   From *The Ring and the Book* 9:

> When here comes tripping Flaccus with his phrase,
> 'Trust me, no miscreant singled from the mob,
> *Crede non illum tibi de scelesta*
> *Plebe delectum.'*

See *Carm.* 2. 4. 17-18:

> Crede non illam tibi de scelesta
> Plebe dilectam.

(12)   From *The Ring and the Book* 9:

> Law that hath listened while the lyrist sang
> *Lene tormentum ingenio admoves,*
> Gently thou joggest by a twinge the wit,
> *Plerumque duro,* else were slow to blab!

See *Carm.* 3. 21. 13-14.

(13)   From *The Ring and the Book* 8:

> Where's a stone?
> *Unde mî lapidem,* where darts for me?
> *Unde sagittas?*

See *Serm.* 2. 7. 116.   (For *mî* read *mihi.*)

(14)   From *The Ring and the Book* 8·

> *Satis superque,* both enough and to spare.

See *Epod.* 1. 31.

(15)   From *The Ring and the Book* 5:

> Nor look that I shall give it, for a grace,
> *Stans pede in uno.*

See *Serm.* 1. 4. 10.

(16)   From *The Ring and the Book* 9:

> *Insanit homo*, threat succeeds to threat

See *Serm.* 2. 7. 117.

(17)   From *The Ring and the Book* 9:

> And thus I end, *tenax proposito.*

See *Carm.* 3. 3. 1: *tenacem propositi.*

(18)   From *The Ring and the Book* 9:

> *Solvuntur tabulae?* May we laugh and go?

See *Serm.* 2. 1. 86:

> Solventur risu tabulae, tu missus abibis.

(19)   From *The Ring and the Book* 9:

> *Quid vetat*, what forbids, I aptly ask,
> With Horace.

See *Serm.* 1. 1. 25 and 1. 10. 56.

(20)   From *The Ring and the Book* 4:

> *Notum tonsoribus!* To the Tonsor then!

See *Serm.* 1. 7. 3:

> Et lippis notum et tonsoribus.

(21)   From *The Ring and the Book* 2:

> Barbers and blear-eyed, as the ancient sings.

See the preceding reference.

(22)   From *The Ring and the Book* 8:

> These are reality, and all else,—fluff,
> Nutshell, and naught,—thank Flaccus for the phrase!

The reference must be to *Serm.* 2. 5. 35-36:

> Eripiet quivis oculos citius mihi, quam te
> Contemptum cassa nuce pauperet.

(23)   From *The Ring and the Book* 8:

> By mutilation of each paramour—
> As Galba in the Horatian satire grieved.

See *Serm.* 1. 2. 45-46 for the reference.

(24)   From *The Ring and the Book* 9:

> Whereupon,
> As Flaccus prompts, I dare the epic plunge.

See *Ars Poet.* 148-149:

> In medias res
> Non secus ac notas auditorem rapit.

(25)   From *The Ring and the Book* 9:

> Say, she kissed him, say, he kissed her again!
> Such osculation was a potent means,
> A very efficacious help, no doubt:
> Such with a third part of her nectar did
> Venus imbue: why should Pompilia fling
> The poet's declaration in his teeth?

See *Carm.* 1. 13. 15-16:

> Oscula, quae Venus
> Quinta parte sui nectaris imbuit.

(The 'third' may be a slip.)

(26)   From *The Ring and the Book* 9:

> O splendidly mendacious!

See *Carm.* 3. 11. 35:

> Splendide mendax.

(27)   From *The Ring and the Book* 2:

> Drop by drop
> Came slow distilment from the alembic here
> Set on to simmer by Canidian hate.

The witch Canidia is often mentioned by Horace, always with the utmost contempt and detestation. See *Epod.* 3, 5, 17; *Serm.* 1. 8, 2. 1, 2. 8.

(28)   From *The Ring and the Book* 3:

> Oh mouse-birth of that mountain-like revenge!

See *Ars Poet.* 139:

> Parturient montes, nascetur ridiculus mus.

Browning has several other references to this same line; for example;

(29)   from *Master Hugues of Saxe-Gotha:*

> Proved a mere mountain in labor;

and

(30)   from *Red Cotton Night-Cap Country* 1:

> Ay, the mother-mouse
> (Reversing fable, as truth can and will)
> Which gave our mountain of a London birth!

(31)   From *Fifine at the Fair*, stanza 82:

> Try if, trusting to sea-tracklessness, I class
> With those around whose breast grew oak and triple brass:
> Who dreaded no degree of death, but, with dry eyes,
> Surveyed the turgid main and its monstrosities—
> And rendered futile so, the prudent Power's decree
> Of separate earth and disassociating sea;
> Since, how is it observed, if impious vessels leap
> Across, and tempt a thing they should not touch—the deep?
> (See Horace to the boat, wherein, for Athens bound,
> When Virgil must embark—Jove keep him safe and sound!—
> The poet bade his friend start on the watery road,
> Much reassured by this so comfortable ode.)

This passage, from line 2 to line 8, is a fairly close translation of
Carm. 1. 3. 9 ff.:

> Illi robur et aes triplex
>   Circa pectus erat.   .   .   .
>   .   .   .   .
> Quem mortis timuit gradum,
>   Qui siccis oculis monstra natantia,
> Qui vidit mare turbidum?   .   .   .
>   .   .   .   .
> Nequiquam deus abscidit
>   Prudens Oceano dissociabili
> Terras, si tamen impiae
>   Non tangenda rates transiliunt vada.

Browning's 'turgid main' is due to his knowledge of the reading
mare turgidum, preferred by some editors.

(32)   From *The Two Poets of Croisic*, stanza 154:

> Did earlier Agamemnons lack their bard?
> But later bards lacked Agamemnon, too!

See *Carm.* 4. 9. 25-28:

> Vixere fortes ante Agamemnona
> Multi; sed omnes inlacrimabiles
>   Urgentur ignotique longa
>   Nocte, carent quia vate sacro.

(33)   From *Imperante Augusto Natus Est:*

> 'Nobody like him [Varius],' little Flaccus laughed,
> 'At leading forth an Epos with due pomp!
> Only, when godlike Caesar swells the theme,
> How should mere mortals hope to praise aright?
> Tell me, thou offshoot of Etruscan kings!'
> Whereat Maecenas smiling sighed assent.

See *Serm.* 1. 10. 43-44:

> Forte epos acer,
> Ut nemo, Varius ducit;

and *Carm.* 3. 29. 1-3:

> Tyrrhena regum progenies,   .   .   .
>   .   .   .   Maecenas.

(34)   From *White Witchcraft:*

> Now say your worst, Canidia!

See above, No. 27, for Horace's references to Canidia.

(35)   From an undated letter to Mr. Fox:

> 'A free and easy sort of thing which he wrote some months ago "on one leg." '

See *Serm.* 1. 4. 9-10:

> In hora saepe ducentos,
> Ut magnum, versus dictabat stans pede in uno.

(36)   From a letter to Dr. Furnivall, 1882:

> 'The *ridiculus mus* is the inveterate nibbler at, and spoiler of, a man's whole life's labor.'

See *Ars Poet.* 139.

(37)   From a letter to Elizabeth Barrett, March 3, 1846:

> 'Milnes said I was the only literary man he ever knew, *tenax propositi*, able to make out a life for himself and abide in it.'

See *Carm.* 3. 3. 1: *tenacem propositi.*

(38)   From a letter to Mr. Fox, April 16, 1835:

> 'A fit compeer of the potter in Horace who anticipated an amphora and produced a porridge-pot.'

See *Ars Poet.* 21-22:

> Amphora coepit
> Institui; currente rota cur urceus exit?

(39)   From an autograph album, inscribed under

> Omnibus hoc vitium est cantoribus, inter amicos
> Ut numquam inducant animum cantare rogati,
> Iniussi numquam desistant.
>
> [*Serm.* 1. 3. 1-3]:

> All singers, trust me, have this common vice,
> To sing 'mid friends you'll have to ask them twice.
> If you don't ask them 'tis another thing,
> Until the judgment day be sure they'll sing.

(40)   From *Imperante Augusto Natus Est:*

> Well may the poet-people each with each
> Vie in his [Caesar's] praise, our company of swans,
> Virgil and Horace, singers—in their way—
> Nearly as good as Varius, though less famed:
> Well may they cry, 'No mortal, plainly God!'

Horace celebrates Augustus many times. The idea of the emperor's divinity may be found in *Carm.* 1. 2. 41-45:

> Sive mutata iuvenem figura
> Ales in terris imitaris almae
> Filius Maiae, patiens vocari
>   Caesaris ultor,
> Serus in caelum redeas;

in *Carm.* 3. 3. 11-12:

> Quos inter Augustus recumbens
> Purpureo bibet ore nectar;

and in *Carm.* 3. 5. 2-3:

> Praesens divus habebitur
> Augustus.

Browning was not judging the poets in his own person, but under the assumed guise of their Roman contemporary.

For the sake of completeness I append one or two colorless references:

(41)   From *The Ring and the Book* 1:

> Vulgarized Horace for the use of schools.

(42) From *Parleyings with Certain People of Importance* (*Parleyings with Christopher Smart*, stanza 8):

> Smart's who translated Horace.

II. *Probable traces of Horace*

(1) From *Pauline:*

> Such lays
> As straight encircle men with praise and love,
> So I should not die utterly.

See *Carm.* 3. 30. 6 (referring to the immortality of verse):

> Non omnis moriar.

(2) From *The Ring and the Book* 9:

> 'Tis Guido henceforth guides Pompilia's step,
> Cries, 'No more friskings o'er the fruitful glebe.'
> . . . .
> We seek not there should lapse the natural law,
> The proper piety to lord and king
> And husband: let the heifer bear the yoke!

See *Carm.* 2. 5. 1 ff.:

> Nondum subacta ferre iugum valet
> Cervice. . . . .
> Circa virentis est animus tuae
> Campos iuvencae.

(3) From *The Ring and the Book* 12:

> Who knows,
> On what pretence of busy idleness?

See *Epist.* 1. 11. 28:

> Strenua nos exercet inertia.

(4) From *The Ring and the Book* 9:

> Her own chastity, a triple mail.

See *Carm.* 1. 3. 9: *aes triplex.*

(5) From *Sordello* 2:

> His Highness knew what poets were: in brief,
> Had not the tetchy race prescriptive right
> To peevishness, caprice?

See *Epist.* 2. 2. 102: *genus irritabile vatum.*

(6) From *The First-Born of Egypt:*

> Israel's God, whose red hand had avenged
> His servants' cause so fearfully.

See *Carm.* 1. 2. 2-3: *pater . . . rubente dextera.*

(7) From a letter to Elizabeth Barrett, March 30, 1846 (referring to *A Soul's Tragedy*):

> Filing is quite another process from hammering, and a more difficult one. Note that 'filing' is the wrong word.

See *Ars Poet.* 290-291:

> Si non offenderet unum
> Quemque poetarum limae labor et mora.

LIST OF BOOKS CONSULTED

Allingham, H., and Radford, D. (editors). *William Allingham: a Diary*. London, 1907.

Allsop, Thomas. *Letters, Conversations, and Recollections of Samuel Taylor Coleridge*. London, 1864.

Anders, Heinrich R. D. *Shakespeare's Books*. Berlin, 1904.

Asanger, Florian. *Percy Bysshe Shelley's Sprach-Studien: seine Uebersetzungen aus dem Lateinischen und Griechischen*. Bonn, 1911.

Babbitt, Irving. *Masters of Modern French Criticism*. Boston, 1912.

Bettany, W. A. Lewis (compiler). *Confessions of Lord Byron*. London, 1905.

Browning, Robert. *Letters* (ed. Wise). London, 1895.

Browning, Robert. *Poetical Works* (ed. Scudder). Boston, 1895.

Browning, Robert [and E. B.]. *New Poems* (ed. Kenyon). London, 1914.

Byron, Lord. *Don Juan* (ed. E. H. Coleridge). London, 1906.

Byron, Lord. *Letters and Journals* (ed. Prothero). London, 1898-1901.

Byron, Lord. *Poetical Works* (ed. E. H. Coleridge). London, 1898-1904.

Byron, Lord. *Poetical Works* (ed. E. H. Coleridge). New York, 1910.

Caine, Hall. *Life of Samuel Taylor Coleridge*. London, 1887.

Calverley, Charles Stuart. *Works*. London, 1901.

Campbell, James Dykes. *Life of Samuel Taylor Coleridge*. London, 1894.

Chesterton, Gilbert Keith. *Robert Browning*. New York, 1903.

Coleridge, Samuel Taylor. *Anima Poetae* (ed. E. H. Coleridge). Boston, 1895.

Coleridge, Samuel Taylor. *Biographia Epistolaris* (ed. Turnbull). London, 1911.

Coleridge, Samuel Taylor. *Biographia Literaria* (ed. Shawcross). Oxford, 1907.

Coleridge, Samuel Taylor. *Complete Poetical Works* (ed. E. H. Coleridge). Oxford, 1912.

Coleridge, Samuel Taylor. *Complete Works* (ed. Shedd). New York, 1853.

Coleridge, Samuel Taylor. *Essays on his own Times* (ed. Sara Coleridge). London, 1850.

Coleridge, Samuel Taylor. *Letters* (ed. E. H. Coleridge). Boston, 1895.

Collins, John Churton. *Illustrations of Tennyson*. London, 1902.

Colvin, Sidney. *Keats*. London, 1887.

Cooper, Lane. *A Concordance to the Poems of William Wordsworth*. London, 1911.

Cunliffe, John William. *The Influence of Seneca on Elizabethan Tragedy*. London, 1893.

Dana, C. L. and J. C. (compilers). *Horace for Modern Readers*. Woodstock (Vermont), 1908.

De Quincey, Thomas. *Works* (ed. Masson). Edinburgh, 1889-1890.

Dowden, Edward. *Life of Percy Bysshe Shelley*. London, 1886.

Droop, E. J. A. *Die Belesenheit Percy Bysshe Shelley's*. Weimar, 1906.

Duff, John Wight. *Literary History of Rome*. New York, 1909.

Ellis, Frederick Startridge. *Lexical Concordance to the Poetical Works of Percy Bysshe Shelley*. London, 1892.

Fuess, Claude M. *Lord Byron as a Satirist in Verse*. New York, 1912.

Fuhrmann, Ludwig. *Die Belesenheit des jungen Byron*. Berlin, 1903.

Gordon, George Stuart (compiler). *English Literature and the Classics*. Oxford, 1912.

Griffin, W. Hall, and Minchin, H. C. *Life of Robert Browning*. London, 1910.

Hodell, Charles Wesley. *The Old Yellow Book*. Washington, 1908.

Hogg, Thomas Jefferson. *Life of Percy Bysshe Shelley*. London, 1858.

Horace. *Odes and Epodes* (ed. Shorey-Laing). Boston, 1911.

Horace. *Satires and Epistles* (ed. Kirkland). Boston, 1902.

Horace. *Works (Scriptores Latini)*. London, 1825.

Horace. *Works* (ed. Wickham). Oxford, 1903-1904. *

Houghton, Lord. *Life and Letters of John Keats*. London, 1867.

Jeaffreson, John Cordy. *The Real Shelley*. London, 1885.

Keats, John. *Letters* (ed. Forman). London, 1895.

Keats, John. *Poetical Works* (ed. Forman). Oxford, 1910.

Keats, John. *Works* (ed. Forman). London, 1883.

Keble, John. *Lectures on Poetry* (tr. Francis). Oxford, 1912.

Lang, Andrew. *Alfred Tennyson*. Edinburgh, 1901.

Lang, Andrew. *Letters to Dead Authors*. New York, 1899.

Letters of Robert Browning and Elizabeth Barrett Barrett. New York, 1899.

Letteers of the Wordsworth Family (ed. Knight). Boston, 1907.

Linemann, Kurt. *Die Belesenheit von William Wordsworth*. Berlin, 1908.

Lonsdale, J., and Lee, S. *Translation of Horace*. London, 1900.

Lucas, Edward Verrall. *Charles Lamb and the Lloyds*. London, 1898.

Manitius, M. *Analekten zur Geschichte des Horaz im Mittelalter*. Göttingen, 1893.

Mayne, Ethel Colburn. *Byron*. London, 1912.

Medwin, Thomas. *Conversations of Lord Byron*. London, 1824.

Menéndez y Pelayo, Marcelius. *Horacio en España*. Madrid, 1885.

Moore, Edward. *Studies in Dante* (first series). Oxford, 1896.

Moore, Thomas. *Life of Byron*. London, 1832.

Mustard, Wilfred Pirt. *Classical Echoes in Tennyson*. New York, 1904.

Orr, Mrs. Sutherland. *Life and Letters of Robert Browning*. Boston, 1891.

Reinsch, Hugo. *Ben Jonsons Poetik und seine Beziehungen zu Horaz*. Erlangen, 1899.

Sellar, William Young. *Horace and the Elegiac Poets*. Oxford, 1892.

Sharp, William. *Life of Robert Browning*. London, 1890.

Shelley, Percy Bysshe. *Letters to Elizabeth Hitchener*. New York, 1908.

Shelley, Percy Bysshe. *Poetical Works* (ed. Forman). London, 1882.

Shelley, Percy Bysshe. *Poetical Works* (ed. Hutchinson). Oxford, 1912.

Shelley, Percy Bysshe. *Prose Works* (ed. Forman). London, 1880.

Skeat, Walter William. Introduction to Vol. 2 of *Works* of Geoffrey Chaucer, Oxford, 1894.

Smart, Christopher. *Translation of Horace* (revised by Buckley). New York, 1859.

Smith, Nowell (compiler). *Wordsworth's Literary Criticism*. London, 1905.

Starick, Paul. *Die Belesenheit von John Keats und die Grundzüge seiner literarischen Kritik*. Berlin, 1910.

Stemplinger, E. *Das Fortleben der horazischen Lyrik seit der Renaissance*. Leipzig, 1906.

Tennyson, Alfred. *Poems* (ed. Warren). Oxford, 1910.

Tennyson, Alfred. *Poetical Works* (ed. Rolfe). Boston, 1898.

*Used in this thesis as a standard text.

Tennyson, Alfred. *Suppressed Poems* (ed. Thomson). New York, 1903.
Tennyson, Alfred. *Works* (ed. H. Tennyson). New York, 1908.
Tennyson, Alfred. *Works* (ed. H. Tennyson). New York, 1913.
Tennyson, Hallam. *Alfred Lord Tennyson: a Memoir.* New York, 1897.
Tucker, Thomas George. *The Foreign Debt of English Literature.* London, 1907.
Tyrrell, Robert Yelverton. *Latin Poetry.* Boston, 1895.
Wordsworth, Christopher. *Memoirs of William Wordsworth* (ed. Reed). Boston, 1851.
Wordsworth, William. *Poems* (ed. Knight). London, 1896.
Wordsworth, William. *Poems* (ed. Smith). London, 1908.
Wordsworth, William. *Poetical Works* (ed. Hutchinson). Oxford, 1910.
Wordsworth, William. *Prose Works* (ed. Knight). London, 1896.

INDEX OF PASSAGES FROM HORACE